CONTENTS

JEREMIAH
BIBLE STUDY SERIES

EPHESIANS

THE INHERITANCE WE HAVE IN CHRIST

DR. DAVID JEREMIAH

Prepared by Peachtree Publishing Services

Harper*Christian*
Resources

Ephesians
Jeremiah Bible Study Series

© 2020 by Dr. David Jeremiah

Requests for information should be addressed to:
HarperChristian Resources, 3900 Sparks Dr. SE, Grand Rapids, Michigan 49546

Published in Nashville, Tennessee, by Thomas Nelson. Thomas Nelson is a registered trademark of HarperCollins Christian Publishing, Inc.

Produced with assistance of Peachtree Publishing Services (www.PeachtreePublishingServices.com). Project staff include Christopher D. Hudson, Randy Southern, and Peter Blankenship.

All Scripture quotations are taken from The Holy Bible, New King James Version. Copyright © 1979, 1980, 1982 by Thomas Nelson. All rights reserved.

ISBN 978-0-310-09168-4 (softcover)
ISBN 978-0-310-09169-1 (ebook)

First Printing May 2020 / Printed in the United States of America
24 25 26 27 28 LBC 11 10 9 8 7

INTRODUCTION TO

The Letter to the Ephesians

"And you He made alive, who were dead in trespasses and sins, in which you once walked according to the course of this world, according to the prince of the power of the air" (Ephesians 2:1–2). Paul wrote these words to believers in Asia Minor, the site of a battle royal taking place between Christianity and Greek and Roman religions. The city of Ephesus, for its part, was home to a temple dedicated to Artemis, a fertility goddess, and her worship involved prostitution and other illicit sexual activity. Other cities in the region had similar temples devoted to one god or another—and believers were feeling the tension between their new faith in Christ and the practices of the culture that surrounded them. So Paul penned this letter to remind them that Jesus was superior to everything the pagan religions had to offer. In fact, they had been spiritually *dead* in their former lives, living under the power of the enemy and sin, but Jesus had set them free and actually returned them to *life*. Paul's words still resonate with believers today, for we also need to know that following Jesus has a point and a purpose—and that life in Christ is far superior to any other way of life the world has to offer.

AUTHOR AND DATE

The writer of the letter identifies himself as "Paul, an apostle of Jesus Christ" (1:1) and "Paul, the prisoner of Christ Jesus" (3:1), and the content, themes, and vocabulary in the epistle share similarities with his other letters. Ignatius of Antioch (c. AD 35–108), an early church father, quotes from the letter in his own writings and indicates that he assumed the author was Paul. The author of Ephesians also claims that he was a prisoner (see 3:1), and this fact aligns with Luke's account in the final chapter of Acts, where he tells of Paul's house arrest in the city of Rome. Given that Ephesians shares many similarities in content to the epistle of Colossians, scholars believe that the two letters were penned at about the same time. This would likely place the date of composition at AD 60, during the time of Paul's arrest in Rome.

BACKGROUND AND SETTING

Paul's letter to the Ephesians was likely circulated to a group of believers in the region of Asia Minor, rather than to the church located in the city. Scholars believe this is true due to the fact that (1) the word *Ephesus* does not appear in the oldest Greek manuscripts, (2) the author reports hearing information about the believers secondhand, and (3) the overall tone of the letter is impersonal in nature. All of these factors would prove to be inconsistent if Paul were directing the letter at a beloved community of believers in a city where he ministered for nearly three years. Unlike most of Paul's other letters, the specific situation that prompted his writing this letter is also unknown. There appears to be no crisis that Paul was addressing and no specific arguments from opponents that he was countering. Most likely, the purpose behind the letter (as with the epistle of Colossians) was to encourage the believers to be united in love and fully understand the blessings of the gift of salvation they had received. As previously noted, Paul was likely in prison in Rome when he wrote the letter, and he was seeking to ground, shape, and challenge his readers long-distance so they would grow in their faith.

KEY THEMES

Several key themes are prominent in the letter to the Ephesians. The first is that *salvation comes through faith alone and is a gift of grace from God*. Paul wanted the believers to understand the incredible riches that they had been given in Christ. They had once been dead in their sins but had now received eternal life. This life in Jesus was far superior to anything the world had to offer (see 1:1–23). Paul also wanted the believers to recognize they were saved not because of anything they had done but because of everything God had done (see 2:1–3:21). Understanding that salvation is a gift, unearned, and freely given, encourages a humble spirit.

A second theme is that *believers in Christ need to be united* (see 4:1–6, 17–31). This was an especially important message for the congregations in the region of Asia Minor, which were comprised of both Jewish and Gentile converts. These two groups had historically been opposed to one another, with Jews considering the Gentiles to be "unclean" and the Gentiles considering the Jewish practices to be strange and unusual. In order to establish unity, the believers needed to get past these ingrained animosities toward one another.

A third theme is that *believers must exercise their spiritual gifts* (see 4:7–16). Paul explains that all believers are given unique spiritual abilities by God. Some people are equipped to be teachers. Others are equipped to be administrators or evangelists. Paul's discussion of these spiritual gifts dovetails with his theme of unity. The apostle makes it clear that the believers' spiritual gifts were intended to be put to use for the benefit of the *entire* body of Christ.

A fourth theme is that *believers must walk in love, light, and wisdom* (see 4:17–6:9). Paul called the Christians in Asia Minor to live in light of all the blessings they had received and conduct themselves in a way that was worthy of their high callings. They were to put off old behaviors that were incompatible with their new life in Christ and serve one another in the body of Christ. They were to imitate God's attribute of love within their communities.

A final theme is that *believers must engage in spiritual warfare* (see 6:10–24). The Christians in Asia Minor were no strangers to Satan's strategies. The pagan activity in Ephesus and the other Roman cities exerted a strong pull on them. Those who resisted were regarded as outcasts and often persecuted for choosing to follow the way of Christ. Paul recognized these attacks against believers as coming directly from the enemy—"The prince of the power of the air, the spirit who now works in the sons of disobedience" (2:2). He encouraged them to recognize they were in a spiritual battle and needed to utilize the armor of God to defend themselves.

KEY APPLICATIONS

Ephesians is one of the most influential documents ever written. In this short letter, Paul calls us to consider all the riches that we have received in Christ and live worthy of our high calling. When we accept Jesus as our Lord and Savior, it should make a profound difference in our lives—for we move from spiritual death and are reborn as completely new creations. Paul asks us to remember that we are set apart by God and should be pursuing His purposes as a unified body. We must also never forget we are in a *spiritual battle*—and "armor up" accordingly each day.

SECURE IN CHRIST

Ephesians 1:1–14

GETTING STARTED

What comes to mind when you hear the word *saint*?

_____

_____

_____

_____

_____

_____

_____

_____

_____

_____

_____

_____

_____

_____

SETTING THE STAGE

Paul begins this letter with an introduction and an address: "Paul, an apostle of Jesus Christ by the will of God, to the saints who are in

Ephesus" (1:1). Paul's use of the term *apostle* (*apostolos* in the Greek) refers to one who has been commissioned by a higher authority to fulfill a particular mission. Paul is consistent in each of his letters in claiming that he was commissioned by Jesus Himself to spread the gospel to the Gentile (non-Jewish) world. Thus, Paul establishes from the beginning of this letter that he is stepping into that role as an apostle, providing the guidance they need to follow so they can mature in their faith.

Paul refers to these believers as *saints*. While this term often brings up images in our minds of venerated figures in church history who have churches and cathedrals named after them, the Greek term that Paul employs (*hagioi*) simply refers to those who have been called to follow Jesus and are faithful in pursuing His ways. In the New Testament, the word almost always appears in the plural, and it always refers to the people of God.

In other words, a *saint* is just another name for a Christian. But Paul's use of the term is especially poignant for the believers in Ephesus. The city at the time rivaled Corinth for its decadence and pagan worship practices. It was one of the filth capitals of the Roman world, and the believers were constantly surrounded by debauchery. Yet Paul reminds them that God had called them out of that cesspool of evil and sin. They had risen from their surroundings—like beautiful lilies on a stagnant pond—and God considered them *saints*.

For believers today, the word *saint* doesn't suggest that we are all perfect or that any of us is better than anyone else. However, it does remind us that we are *set apart* for a higher purpose . . . which is the literal meaning of the word *holy*. All believers in Christ are *saints*—adopted children of God who have been given the blessings of God's eternal kingdom.

EXPLORING THE TEXT

Greeting to the Saints (Ephesians 1:1–6)

[1] Paul, an apostle of Jesus Christ by the will of God,

    To the saints who are in Ephesus, and faithful in Christ Jesus:

² Grace to you and peace from God our Father and the Lord Jesus Christ.

³ Blessed be the God and Father of our Lord Jesus Christ, who has blessed us with every spiritual blessing in the heavenly places in Christ, ⁴ just as He chose us in Him before the foundation of the world, that we should be holy and without blame before Him in love, ⁵ having predestined us to adoption as sons by Jesus Christ to Himself, according to the good pleasure of His will, ⁶ to the praise of the glory of His grace, by which He made us accepted in the Beloved.

1. In his greeting to the believers, Paul not only identifies himself as the author but also establishes his credibility by calling himself an apostle. What does Paul want his readers to understand about his calling as an apostle (see verse 1)?

_____

_____

_____

_____

_____

2. Paul is clear in this passage that God chose these believers and predestined them for spiritual adoption into His family. The word *predestined* implies setting boundaries so that a person stays on a certain course and reaches a specific destination. According to Paul, for what reason does God choose to predestine a person (see verses 4–6)?

_____

_____

_____

_____

_____

Redemption in Christ (Ephesians 1:7–14)

7 In Him we have redemption through His blood, the forgiveness of sins, according to the riches of His grace 8 which He made to abound toward us in all wisdom and prudence, 9 having made known to us the mystery of His will, according to His good pleasure which He purposed in Himself, 10 that in the dispensation of the fullness of the times He might gather together in one all things in Christ, both which are in heaven and which are on earth—in Him. 11 In Him also we have obtained an inheritance, being predestined according to the purpose of Him who works all things according to the counsel of His will, 12 that we who first trusted in Christ should be to the praise of His glory.

13 In Him you also trusted, after you heard the word of truth, the gospel of your salvation; in whom also, having believed, you were sealed with the Holy Spirit of promise, 14 who is the guarantee of our inheritance until the redemption of the purchased possession, to the praise of His glory.

3. The *mystery* that Paul mentions refers to something that is not discoverable through human knowledge or insight. What mystery has God revealed to the believers (see verses 9–10)?

_____

_____

_____

_____

_____

_____

_____

_____

_____

4. Paul reminds the believers that they not only have been chosen by God but also have received a promised *inheritance* from Him (see verses 11–14). Why would this have been important for them to remember, given the temptation they were facing to return to their former ways?

_____

_____

_____

_____

_____

_____

_____

_____

GOING DEEPER

Paul opens his letter to the Ephesians with a typical "thanksgiving" section that he includes in most of his epistles (what scholars refer to as a *doxology*). However, the apostle also picks up on a theme that was found in the Old Testament books of prophecy—that God "works all things according to the counsel of His will" (verse 11). In the following passage, the prophet Isaiah expounds on this idea that God is sovereign and works out all things according to His purposes.

Dead Idols and the Living God (Isaiah 46:8–13)

8 "Remember this, and show yourselves men;
Recall to mind, O you transgressors.
9 Remember the former things of old,
For I am God, and there is no other;
I am God, and there is none like Me,
10 Declaring the end from the beginning,

And from ancient times things that are not yet done,

Saying, 'My counsel shall stand,

And I will do all My pleasure,'

[11] Calling a bird of prey from the east,

The man who executes My counsel, from a far country.

Indeed I have spoken it;

I will also bring it to pass.

I have purposed it;

I will also do it.

[12] "Listen to Me, you stubborn-hearted,

Who are far from righteousness:

[13] I bring My righteousness near, it shall not be far off;

My salvation shall not linger.

And I will place salvation in Zion,

For Israel My glory."

---

5. God calls His people to *recall* and *remember* how He revealed Himself to them in the past (see verses 8–9). What about His nature does God want the people to remember?

_____

_____

_____

_____

_____

_____

_____

_____

_____

_____

_____

6. How does God summarize His sovereignty and His purposes (see verses 10–13)?

_____

_____

_____

_____

_____

_____

_____

_____

Paul not only confirms that God is sovereign but also that He has a perfect plan for His creation. In Ephesians 1:10, he uses the phrase *gather together*, which can also mean "to unite" or "to sum up." In ancient times, it was used to describe the process of adding a column of figures and putting the sum up at the top. Paul thus states that God will make all things "add up" for believers in the end. He reiterates this point in his letter to the Romans.

From Suffering to Glory (Romans 8:18–25)

18 For I consider that the sufferings of this present time are not worthy to be compared with the glory which shall be revealed in us. 19 For the earnest expectation of the creation eagerly waits for the revealing of the sons of God. 20 For the creation was subjected to futility, not willingly, but because of Him who subjected it in hope; 21 because the creation itself also will be delivered from the bondage of corruption into the glorious liberty of the children of God. 22 For we know that the whole creation groans and labors with birth pangs together until now. 23 Not only that, but we also who have the firstfruits of the Spirit, even we ourselves groan within ourselves, eagerly waiting for

the adoption, the redemption of our body. [24] For we were saved in this hope, but hope that is seen is not hope; for why does one still hope for what he sees? [25] But if we hope for what we do not see, we eagerly wait for it with perseverance.

---

7. How does Paul put into perspective "the sufferings of this present time"? How does Paul compare creation in its present state with the glory that is to come (see verses 18–22)?

_____

_____

_____

_____

_____

_____

_____

_____

8. Paul uses the process of birth as a picture of the hope we have in Christ. How does hoping for "what [you] do not see" affect the way you live (see verses 22–25)?

_____

_____

_____

_____

_____

_____

_____

_____

Reviewing the Story

Paul begins his letter by explaining the riches of God—a wealth that cannot be lost. He emphasizes that God is the giver of every spiritual blessing and that Christians are the recipients. To help the Ephesian believers understand what this means, he lists eight different spiritual blessings: they have been chosen, adopted, accepted, redeemed, enlightened, given an inheritance, sealed, and secured. Paul wants the believers to understand their identity in Christ and exactly what it means to be chosen by God.

9. What has God done for us (see Ephesians 1:3)?

10. When did God choose us? What was His purpose in choosing us (see Ephesians 1:4)?

11. What do we have in Christ (see Ephesians 1:7)?

_____

_____

_____

_____

_____

_____

12. What role does the Holy Spirit play in our lives as believers (see Ephesians 1:13–14)?

_____

_____

_____

_____

_____

_____

APPLYING THE MESSAGE

13. List the blessings that stand out to you from Ephesians 1:1–14. Why are they so meaningful to you?

_____

_____

_____

_____

_____

_____

_____

14. How does knowing that you have an eternal inheritance help you face trials in this life?

_____

_____

_____

_____

_____

_____

REFLECTING ON THE MEANING

The story is told of an old man who was asked to give his testimony in his church. He was excited about the opportunity, and when he got up, he talked about God until he couldn't think of anything more to say. He spoke at length about how God had loved him, called him, found him, cleansed him, and filled him. He gave a glorious testimony.

At the end of the service, he was approached by a younger man in the congregation who felt it was his duty to provide some correction. He came up to the old man and said, "I liked your testimony . . . except you just talked about God's part. You didn't tell us about your part. Salvation is a two-way deal. You've got to do your part, and God has got to do His part. We only heard about God's part. Why didn't you tell us about _your_ part?" The old man thought about this for a moment. "Well, I guess I should," he said. "I'll tell you what my part was. I ran away from God as fast as I could, and He ran after me. That's the way it worked."

This is the way that it worked for most of us. We didn't come begging to God. Rather, God came after us and pursued us until He made us His own. As a result, we now know that we are adopted into His family, accepted in His Beloved, redeemed, and forgiven . . . and that we have an eternal inheritance in store for us. God chose us in Christ "before the foundation of the world" (Ephesians 1:4). From eternity past to eternity future, we are in Christ.

JOURNALING YOUR RESPONSE

How did God pursue you and lead you to put your faith in Christ?

A PRAYER FOR EMPOWERMENT

Ephesians 1:15–23

GETTING STARTED

Why is it often so easy to take God's blessings in our lives for granted?

_____

_____

_____

_____

_____

_____

_____

_____

_____

_____

_____

_____

_____

_____

_____

_____

_____

SETTING THE STAGE

Many visitors to the West Coast have toured Hearst Castle, the home of the late newspaper publisher William Randolph Hearst. If you have ever been through that home, you know the great fondness that Hearst had for art treasures from around the world. For Hearst, this passion for collecting was driven by an insatiable desire to possess more and more.

The story is told that one day when Hearst was reading an art catalog, he found descriptions of some valuable items. Money was not an issue, so he brought in his agent and told him to go wherever he had to go in order to find the items. The agent visited several countries, but was unable to find them. Finally, he sent a telegram to Hearst, telling him he had found the items. It turned out that they were in Hearst's own warehouse.

In the previous section of the letter to the Ephesians, the apostle Paul reminded the believers that they were rich according to the standards of heaven. They had been adopted, accepted, redeemed, given an inheritance in heaven, and sealed by the Holy Spirit. But did they recognize the extent of the blessings they had been given? Or were they overlooking these blessings—not recognizing the valuable treasure they had in their own spiritual "warehouses"?

Paul was not content to just tell the believers about these blessings. He desired for them to acknowledge and receive these blessings so they could use them for God's glory. His prayer in this next section of his letter is for the Ephesians—and us—to experience all the things that he has been talking about. We need to embrace these truths in our hearts.

EXPLORING THE TEXT

Paul's Prayer for the Ephesians (Ephesians 1:15–18)

¹⁵ Therefore I also, after I heard of your faith in the Lord Jesus and your love for all the saints, ¹⁶ do not cease to give thanks for you, making mention of you in my prayers: ¹⁷ that the God of our Lord Jesus

Christ, the Father of glory, may give to you the spirit of wisdom and revelation in the knowledge of Him, [18] the eyes of your understanding being enlightened . . .

1. Paul states he has *heard* reports of these believers, which indicates the letter was circulated to a region and not just sent to the church in Ephesus, where he had ministered for nearly three years. What in particular has Paul heard about them (see verses 15–16)?

_____

_____

_____

_____

_____

2. What does Paul pray that God would give to these believers (see verses 17–18)?

_____

_____

_____

_____

_____

Prayer for Spiritual Wisdom (Ephesians 1:18–23)

. . . that you may know what is the hope of His calling, what are the riches of the glory of His inheritance in the saints, [19] and what is the exceeding greatness of His power toward us who believe, according to the working of His mighty power [20] which He worked in Christ when He raised Him from the dead and seated Him at His right hand in the heavenly places, ²¹ far above all principality and power and might and dominion, and every name that is named, not only in this age but also in that which is to come. ²² And He put all things under His feet, and gave Him to be head over all things to the church, ²³ which is His body, the fullness of Him who fills all in all.

---

3. Paul prays that the believers would recognize God's calling on their lives, comprehend the riches they have been given as an inheritance, and experience God's power. How does he explain the power that he has asked God to provide for them (see verses 18–20)?

_____

_____

_____

_____

_____

4. How does Paul describe Jesus' authority (see verses 21–23)? What confidence and comfort would this have given to these believers who were fighting unseen spiritual battles around them?

_____

_____

_____

_____

_____

GOING DEEPER

At the center of the apostle Paul's prayer in this opening section of his letter to the Ephesians is the remarkable truth that believers in Christ are God's *inheritance*. As Paul writes, his desire is for the believers to "know what is the hope of His calling, what are the riches of the glory of His inheritance in the saints, and what is the exceeding greatness of His power toward us who believe" (verses 18–19). God sees us as a treasure—as His special inheritance! Centuries earlier, another writer marveled at this same truth when he penned the words of the following psalm.

Let God's People Rejoice (Psalm 149:1–9)

[1] Praise the LORD!

Sing to the LORD a new song,
And His praise in the assembly of saints.

[2] Let Israel rejoice in their Maker;
Let the children of Zion be joyful in their King.
[3] Let them praise His name with the dance;
Let them sing praises to Him with the timbrel and harp.
[4] For the LORD takes pleasure in His people;
He will beautify the humble with salvation.

[5] Let the saints be joyful in glory;
Let them sing aloud on their beds.
[6] Let the high praises of God be in their mouth,
And a two-edged sword in their hand,
[7] To execute vengeance on the nations,
And punishments on the peoples;
[8] To bind their kings with chains,
And their nobles with fetters of iron;
[9] To execute on them the written judgment—
This honor have all His saints.

Praise the LORD!

5. What titles, characteristics, and actions of God does the psalmist include in this passage?

_____

_____

_____

_____

_____

6. How should God's people respond to who God is and what He has done? How do your attitudes and actions demonstrate your "high praises of God" (verse 6)?

_____

_____

_____

_____

_____

Paul is thankful for the believers in the region of Ephesus not just because of their love for God but also because of their "love for all the saints" (verse 15). The evidence of God's work in us is not just the love we claim to have for Him but the love we have for His people. Paul here is emphasizing a point that Jesus made to His disciples, as recorded in the Gospel of John.

The New Commandment (John 13:31–35)

31 So, when he had gone out, Jesus said, "Now the Son of Man is glorified, and God is glorified in Him. 32 If God is glorified in Him, God will also glorify Him in Himself, and glorify Him immediately. 33 Little children, I shall be with you a little while longer. You will seek Me; and as I said to the Jews, 'Where I am going, you cannot come,' so now I say to you. 34 A new commandment I give to you, that you love one another; as I have loved you, that you also love

one another. ³⁵ By this all will know that you are My disciples, if you have love for one another."

---

7. Jesus made this statement when He was preparing His disciples for His departure from them. He knew His mission on earth was coming to an end, so He gave them important final instructions on how they were to love one another and follow Him even after He was gone. What standard of love did Jesus set for His disciples and for us (see verse 34)?

_____

_____

_____

_____

8. How did Jesus say people would recognize His disciples (see verse 35)? In what ways can you be more intentional about following Jesus' commandment to love all the saints?

_____

_____

_____

REVIEWING THE STORY

Paul's reflection on the gift of God's blessings—and the reports he has heard of the believers' love for the saints—compels him to write a prayer of thanksgiving. He prays that God will give the believers a spirit of wisdom, that they will come to understand His truths, and that they will realize the riches they have been given in Christ. Paul also prays they will receive the same power that God worked to raise Jesus from the dead. He reminds the believers that the resurrected Christ they serve is above all the principalities and powers of this world.

9. What reports had the apostle Paul heard about the Ephesians (see Ephesians 1:15)?

_____

_____

_____

_____

_____

10. What type of wisdom does Paul want God to provide to them (see Ephesians 1:17–18)?

_____

_____

_____

_____

_____

_____

11. How does Paul describe the power he wanted them to receive (see Ephesians 1:19–21)?

_____

_____

_____

_____

_____

_____

12. What does Paul state about Jesus' authority (see Ephesians 1:21–22)?

_____

_____

_____

_____

_____

APPLYING THE MESSAGE

13. What are some problems you are facing right now that you need God's wisdom to solve?

_____

_____

_____

_____

14. In what areas of life would you like to receive more of God's power?

_____

_____

_____

REFLECTING ON THE MEANING

Paul's prayer for the believers—and for us—is to receive the power that God "worked in Christ when He raised Him from the dead" (Ephesians 1:20). What can this type of power accomplish in our world? First, _God's power can rescue any person from sin._ The power that raised Jesus from the dead secured His victory over sin and death. Our Lord is able to rescue _anyone,_ regardless of their past mistakes, when they choose to put their faith in Him.

Furthermore, God wants to exhibit His power in people's lives. As we discover in the Bible, He finds those who are humbled by their past mistakes and lifts them up, bringing them into a saving relationship and using them to change the world. As the author of Hebrews states, "He is also able to save to the uttermost those who come to God through Him" (Hebrews 7:25). No one is beyond God's rescue, for He is _able_ to save all. No matter who we are or what we have done, God can lift us up. We can become part of His family.

Second, _God's power can recover any saint._ The power of God not only meets our spiritual needs, but it meets our physical needs as well. Sadly, many

21

believers today dismiss this power of God in their lives. They act like people whom God has cured of cancer but who can't trust Him to heal their arthritis. If God has already done the biggest thing by forgiving our sins, surely we can trust Him to provide for our everyday needs and restore us when we fall.

The same power that God used to save us is the power He wants to use to restore us to a place of health and happiness. Again, as the author of Hebrews states, "For in that He Himself has suffered, being tempted, He is able to aid those who are tempted" (2:18). God is waiting for us to say, "Lord, you saved me. Now help me through these financial troubles, help me through these physical problems, help me overcome this temptation."

When we call on the name of the Lord, we can be certain that He has the power to answer our prayer.

Journaling Your Response

What is a situation in your life right now that you need to bring before God—and believe that He is willing and able to answer your prayer?

ALIVE IN CHRIST

Ephesians 2:1–13

GETTING STARTED

What circumstances prompted you to give your life to Christ?

_____

_____

_____

_____

_____

_____

_____

_____

_____

_____

_____

_____

SETTING THE STAGE

Years ago, a group of miners in Chile became trapped 2,300 feet below ground in a mine shaft. The men had no way of extricating themselves, so they were forced to wait in the darkness for help to arrive from above. The miners didn't know it at the time, but they were not waiting alone. Their drama unfolded in real time on the international stage. Across the world, people followed the round-the-clock media coverage of the miners' plight.

Imagine for a minute what it must have been like to be among that group down in the mine. There was absolutely nothing they could do to free themselves. They were completely dependent on someone from above to do something to rescue them. As millions of people watched, this help finally arrived in the form of a specially designed drill bit that could bore a hole to where the miners were trapped. After two months of waiting in the darkness, the men were finally freed and brought to the surface.

This is an ideal picture of salvation. All of us were lost, helpless, and hopeless. We were trapped in the darkness by our sin. There was nothing we could do to free ourselves. If God did not reach down to us, we would have been left in our hopeless state. Paul wanted the believers to understand this truth. Previously, he wrote about the blessings they had received in Christ. Now, he will expound on those blessings and show how different their lives are now that they have received Christ and been "brought to the surface" through His sacrifice.

We can think of this section of the letter as Paul's before-and-after advertisement. Previously, the believers had been spiritually dead and trapped in the darkness of their sin. But now, they were alive in Christ and could experience the wonders of His light. In the process, Paul offers perhaps the most concise presentation of the Christian gospel in the Bible.

EXPLORING THE TEXT

New Life in Christ (Ephesians 2:1–10)

¹ And you He made alive, who were dead in trespasses and sins, ² in which you once walked according to the course of this world, according to the prince of the power of the air, the spirit who now works in the sons of disobedience, ³ among whom also we all once conducted ourselves in the lusts of our flesh, fulfilling the desires

of the flesh and of the mind, and were by nature children of wrath, just as the others.

⁴ But God, who is rich in mercy, because of His great love with which He loved us, ⁵ even when we were dead in trespasses, made us alive together with Christ (by grace you have been saved), ⁶ and raised us up together, and made us sit together in the heavenly places in Christ Jesus, ⁷ that in the ages to come He might show the exceeding riches of His grace in His kindness toward us in Christ Jesus. ⁸ For by grace you have been saved through faith, and that not of yourselves; it is the gift of God, ⁹ not of works, lest anyone should boast. ¹⁰ For we are His workmanship, created in Christ Jesus for good works, which God prepared beforehand that we should walk in them.

---

1. Paul begins by focusing on the transformation that God accomplishes in the lives of those who choose to follow Christ. How does Paul describe our spiritual condition before coming to Christ? What were our desires and motivations (see verses 1–3)?

_____

_____

_____

_____

2. Paul reminds us that no human effort or works can merit salvation. At the same time, we have been created for good works. What should our motivation be for any good works we do? How do these works demonstrate our status as a child of God (see verses 4–9)?

_____

_____

_____

_____

Reconciled Through Christ (Ephesians 2:11–13)

¹¹ Therefore remember that you, once Gentiles in the flesh—who are called Uncircumcision by what is called the Circumcision made in the flesh by hands—¹² that at that time you were without Christ, being aliens from the commonwealth of Israel and strangers from the covenants of promise, having no hope and without God in the world. ¹³ But now in Christ Jesus you who once were far off have been brought near by the blood of Christ.

3. Paul uses the term *uncircumcision* to remind his readers (who were primarily non-Jewish) about what their lives were like before they came to Christ. What example does Paul use to point out the extent of their separation from God (see verses 11–12)?

_____

_____

_____

_____

4. In the Old Testament sacrificial system, the blood of animals was shed to gain forgiveness for sin. While the Gentiles were formerly estranged from God and did not participate in the sacrificial practices of the Jews, they are now "brought near by the blood of Christ" (verse 13). How does the blood of Jesus draw people—both Jews and Gentiles—near to God?

_____

_____

_____

_____

_____

GOING DEEPER

The apostle Paul is clear that it is God, out of His great mercy, who reaches down and rescues humans from their sin. In the Old Testament, we find an example of God doing this in the story of Noah. At the time, humanity had become so wicked that God determined to wipe out the human race. But He chose to reach down and spare one righteous man and his family from this judgment.

God's Plan of Rescue (Genesis 6:5–22)

⁵ Then the LORD saw that the wickedness of man was great in the earth, and that every intent of the thoughts of his heart was only evil continually. ⁶ And the LORD was sorry that He had made man on the earth, and He was grieved in His heart. ⁷ So the LORD said, "I will destroy man whom I have created from the face of the earth, both man and beast, creeping thing and birds of the air, for I am sorry that I have made them." ⁸ But Noah found grace in the eyes of the LORD.

⁹ This is the genealogy of Noah. Noah was a just man, perfect in his generations. Noah walked with God. ¹⁰ And Noah begot three sons: Shem, Ham, and Japheth.

¹¹ The earth also was corrupt before God, and the earth was filled with violence. ¹² So God looked upon the earth, and indeed it was corrupt; for all flesh had corrupted their way on the earth.

¹³ And God said to Noah, "The end of all flesh has come before Me, for the earth is filled with violence through them; and behold, I will destroy them with the earth. ¹⁴ Make yourself an ark of gopherwood; make rooms in the ark, and cover it inside and outside with pitch. ¹⁵ And this is how you shall make it: The length of the ark shall be three hundred cubits, its width fifty cubits, and its height thirty cubits. ¹⁶ You shall make a window for the ark, and you shall finish it to a cubit from above; and set the door of the

ark in its side. You shall make it with lower, second, and third decks. [17] And behold, I Myself am bringing floodwaters on the earth, to destroy from under heaven all flesh in which is the breath of life; everything that is on the earth shall die. [18] But I will establish My covenant with you; and you shall go into the ark—you, your sons, your wife, and your sons' wives with you. [19] And of every living thing of all flesh you shall bring two of every sort into the ark, to keep them alive with you; they shall be male and female. [20] Of the birds after their kind, of animals after their kind, and of every creeping thing of the earth after its kind, two of every kind will come to you to keep them alive. [21] And you shall take for yourself of all food that is eaten, and you shall gather it to yourself; and it shall be food for you and for them."

[22] Thus Noah did; according to all that God commanded him, so he did.

---

5. What caused God to make the decision to wipe out humanity from the earth? What made Him decide to spare Noah and his family from judgment (see verses 5–9)?

_____

_____

_____

_____

_____

_____

_____

_____

_____

_____

_____

6. God was about to execute His plan of judgment on the human race, but He also had a plan for their salvation. What was this plan (see verses 14–18)? How does this story support what Paul says about the way that God has rescued each of us from judgment?

_____

_____

_____

_____

_____

_____

_____

Paul writes that it is by grace we "have been saved through faith . . . not of works" (Ephesians 2:8–9). However, the hallmark of a Christian is to *desire* to do good works as a demonstration of a changed nature—and in appreciation of the gift of life that God has given. James, in his epistle, also stresses the importance of Christians doing good works. While he agrees that such works cannot save a person from sin, he also insists they indicate that an individual has a *living* and *active* faith.

Faith and Works (James 2:14–24)

¹⁴ What does it profit, my brethren, if someone says he has faith but does not have works? Can faith save him? ¹⁵ If a brother or sister is naked and destitute of daily food, ¹⁶ and one of you says to them, "Depart in peace, be warmed and filled," but you do not give them the things which are needed for the body, what does it profit? ¹⁷ Thus also faith by itself, if it does not have works, is dead.

¹⁸ But someone will say, "You have faith, and I have works." Show me your faith without your works, and I will show you my faith by my works. ¹⁹ You believe that there is one God. You do well. Even the demons believe—and tremble! ²⁰ But do you want to know, O

foolish man, that faith without works is dead? [21] Was not Abraham our father justified by works when he offered Isaac his son on the altar? [22] Do you see that faith was working together with his works, and by works faith was made perfect? [23] And the Scripture was fulfilled which says, "Abraham believed God, and it was accounted to him for righteousness." And he was called the friend of God. [24] You see then that a man is justified by works, and not by faith only.

---

7. How does James describe a faith that is "dead"? Although salvation comes through faith alone, why is it critical for Christians also to do good works for others (see verses 14–20)?

_____

_____

_____

_____

_____

_____

8. What point is James making about faith and works by drawing on the example of Abraham? How did Abraham choose to put his faith in action to obey the Lord (see verses 21–24)?

_____

_____

_____

_____

_____

_____

_____

REVIEWING THE STORY

Paul points out the past, present, and future of all believers. In the *past*, we were dead in our sins, deceived by Satan, disobedient to God, defiled by our desires, and doomed by our unrighteousness. But God, in the *present*, reached down and offered us a way to salvation. He did this solely on the basis of His grace, mercy, and love—for there was nothing we could do on our own to escape the judgment for our sins. Now that we have accepted Jesus as our Savior, we have a *future* that includes being seated with Christ in the heavenly places.

9. What was our state before accepting God's gift of salvation (see Ephesians 2:2–3)?

_____

_____

_____

_____

_____

10. What motivated God to reach down and rescue us (see Ephesians 2:4–5)?

_____

_____

_____

_____

_____

11. What does Paul state that believers in Christ were created to do (see Ephesians 2:10)?

_____

_____

_____

_____

_____

_____

12. What illustration from the Old Testament does Paul use to demonstrate our separation from God (see Ephesians 2:12–13)?

_____

_____

_____

_____

_____

APPLYING THE MESSAGE

13. How would you describe the difference in your life since choosing to follow Christ?

_____

_____

_____

_____

_____

_____

_____

14. When have you been tempted to believe that you could somehow earn God's favor through your good works? Why is this a pointless and impossible endeavor?

_____

_____

_____

_____

_____

_____

_____

REFLECTING ON THE MEANING

Paul is clear that we are not saved *by* good works but *for* good works. In other words, we cannot be saved by doing good things, but God expects us to do good things after we are saved—and He gives us the power of the Holy Spirit to accomplish great things on His behalf. This is a principle that Jesus gave to His own disciples on earth when He said, "By this My Father is glorified, that you bear much fruit; so you will be My disciples" (John 15:8).

God wants us to bear fruit for Him—and this naturally involves doing good works for others. As James bluntly states, this is the difference between having a *living* and a *dead* faith—and dead faith does no one any good. Thus, anyone who becomes a Christian and does not change is not really a Christian. This is not a human judgment, for the Bible makes it clear that when God's nature comes into us, we start living differently.

As Paul declares, "We are His workmanship, created in Christ Jesus for good works, which God prepared beforehand that we should walk in them" (Ephesians 2:10). The word translated as *workmanship* comes from the Greek word *poiema*, from which we get the word *poem*. God has saved us, rescued us, and given us new life . . . and now we are to be His literary masterpiece. He wants us to live our lives as an exquisite poem to bring honor and glory to Him.

JOURNALING YOUR RESPONSE

What are some of the good works you believe God has prepared for you?
How can you "walk in" those good works?

A CALL FOR PEACE

Ephesians 2:14–22

GETTING STARTED

Why is it so important for believers in Christ to live in peace with one another? Why is it so challenging?

_____

_____

_____

_____

_____

_____

_____

_____

_____

_____

_____

_____

_____

_____

_____

_____

_____

_____

_____

SETTING THE STAGE

It is hard for us today to comprehend the tension that existed in the early church when Jews *and* Gentiles began to receive Jesus as their Savior. The two groups had historically been opposed to one another. The Jews held the Gentiles to be "unclean" and referred to them as "dogs." Some Jewish women would even refuse to help Gentile women give birth because they didn't want to bring another despised Gentile into the world. The Gentiles, in turn, held the Jews in contempt, ostracized them, and even persecuted them for their beliefs.

Given this tension, you can imagine how the early Jewish converts felt as they witnessed the gospel going to the Gentile nations. They watched as those whom they considered to be pagans began to receive Christ. Not only that, but these Gentiles also began to attend church—with the Jewish believers. It was likely this tension that prompted Paul in the opening section of his letter to remind the believers of how God had reconciled them to Himself. He wanted them to consider the riches they had received through God's grace and remember that they had been called to lead a new life as His chosen saints.

In light of that new life, Paul will now call on the believers to consider how the gift of their salvation should not only impact their own lives but also their interactions with one another. Paul is clear that God didn't save them just so they could live as isolated individual believers or members of their former "cliques." God's plan included bringing *all* people together and uniting men and women from diverse backgrounds. For this reason, there should be peace in their communities—a peace based on Christ.

When we receive salvation, we become new creations in Christ. However, sometimes it still takes a while to get the old baggage out of our lives. Some of our old prejudices can hang around if we don't take the necessary steps to change our mindset, attitudes, and actions. Paul's call in this next section is for us to invite the Holy Spirit to start that work in our lives. For it is only when this transformation occurs that we can achieve peace in the body of Christ.

EXPLORING THE TEXT

Christ Our Peace (Ephesians 2:14–18)

[14] For He Himself is our peace, who has made both one, and has broken down the middle wall of separation, [15] having abolished in His flesh the enmity, that is, the law of commandments contained in ordinances, so as to create in Himself one new man from the two, thus making peace, [16] and that He might reconcile them both to God in one body through the cross, thereby putting to death the enmity. [17] And He came and preached peace to you who were afar off and to those who were near. [18] For through Him we both have access by one Spirit to the Father.

1. Paul uses the word *peace* seven times in his letter to the Ephesians. What does Paul say that Jesus accomplished at the cross? What did He destroy that enables there to be peace among believers (see verses 14–16)?

_____

_____

_____

_____

_____

_____

_____

_____

_____

_____

_____

_____

_____

_____

_____

2. The Greek term that Paul uses for *access* in verse 18 also means a "way of approach." Paul emphasizes there is only one way to approach the Father—and it is not through keeping the law or accomplishing good works. How do Jesus and the Holy Spirit provide the only means of access to the Father (see verses 17–18; see also Ephesians 1:13–14)?

_____

_____

_____

_____

_____

Christ Our Cornerstone (Ephesians 2:19–22)

¹⁹ Now, therefore, you are no longer strangers and foreigners, but fellow citizens with the saints and members of the household of God, ²⁰ having been built on the foundation of the apostles and prophets, Jesus Christ Himself being the chief cornerstone, ²¹ in whom the whole building, being fitted together, grows into a holy temple in the Lord, ²² in whom you also are being built together for a dwelling place of God in the Spirit.

3. Paul notes that because Jesus has broken down the walls that previously separated people, everyone now has access to God. What does Paul say this means for Gentile believers (which includes us)? What standing do we have before God (see verse 19)?

_____

_____

_____

_____

4. In ancient times, a cornerstone determined not only the strength of a building's foundation but also its structure. How does Paul apply this imagery to Jesus as the cornerstone of the church? How would this have contributed to his argument that Jewish and Gentile believers needed to be united since they were part of the same structure (see verses 20–22)?

_____

_____

_____

_____

_____

_____

_____

_____

_____

_____

_____

GOING DEEPER

In this section of his letter, the apostle Paul compels his readers to live in peace with one another because they are all part of a body that is founded on the "cornerstone" of Christ—who is our perfect peace. In making this call to unity, Paul is drawing on imagery of God's peace that was often employed by Old Testament prophets, such as the following from Isaiah.

The Beauty of Peace (Isaiah 52:7–10)

> 7 How beautiful upon the mountains
> Are the feet of him who brings good news,
> Who proclaims peace,
> Who brings glad tidings of good things,

Who proclaims salvation,

Who says to Zion,

"Your God reigns!"

8 Your watchmen shall lift up their voices,

With their voices they shall sing together;

For they shall see eye to eye

When the LORD brings back Zion.

9 Break forth into joy, sing together,

You waste places of Jerusalem!

For the LORD has comforted His people,

He has redeemed Jerusalem.

10 The LORD has made bare His holy arm

In the eyes of all the nations;

And all the ends of the earth shall see

The salvation of our God.

---

5. How does the prophet Isaiah describe the one who brings peace (see verse 7)? What impact would this imagery have had on the early believers who were *not* living at peace?

_____

_____

_____

_____

_____

_____

_____

_____

_____

_____

_____

_____

6. What is the result when the "watchmen" receive this bearer of peace (see verse 8)? How would this apply to the believers whom Paul was addressing in his letter?

_____

_____

_____

_____

_____

Paul was not alone in his call for Christians to live at peace. In the epistle of James, the author echoes this admonition and calls on believers to consider the disastrous impact of divisions between people. As he notes in the following passage, the quarrels and fights that break out between Christian brothers and sisters can actually be traced to division caused by _sin_.

Pride Promotes Strife (James 4:1–6)

¹ Where do wars and fights come from among you? Do they not come from your desires for pleasure that war in your members? ² You lust and do not have. You murder and covet and cannot obtain. You fight and war. Yet you do not have because you do not ask. ³ You ask and do not receive, because you ask amiss, that you may spend it on your pleasures. ⁴ Adulterers and adulteresses! Do you not know that friendship with the world is enmity with God? Whoever therefore wants to be a friend of the world makes himself an enemy of God. ⁵ Or do you think that the Scripture says in vain, "The Spirit who dwells in us yearns jealously"?

⁶ But He gives more grace. Therefore He says:

"God resists the proud,
But gives grace to the humble."

7. James describes the sinfulness that causes people to fight and quarrel—even within a community of believers. What are some of the consequences for the church—the people of God—embracing a friendship with the world (see verses 1–4)?

_____

_____

_____

_____

_____

8. How does the Holy Spirit, who dwells within the church, provide a way to avoid divisions within congregations of believers (see verses 5–6)?

_____

_____

_____

_____

_____

_____

REVIEWING THE STORY

Paul reminds his mixed congregations of Jewish and Gentile believers that they were once *all* separated from God but now—through Christ—can achieve peace with Him. He calls on them to remember that Jesus has broken down the barriers that separated them and for them to model this same behavior in their interactions with one another. Paul then uses the analogy of Jesus as a cornerstone to show how believers should be "building" the church. The church is a place where all are accepted and being "fitted together" for use in God's service to the world.

9. How does the apostle Paul describe Jesus (see Ephesians 2:14–15)?

_____

_____

_____

_____

_____

_____

_____

_____

10. What did Jesus accomplish for Jews and Gentiles through the cross (see Ephesians 2:16)?

_____

_____

_____

_____

_____

_____

_____

_____

11. What were Gentiles considered to be before they became fellow citizens with the saints and members of the household of God (see Ephesians 2:19)?

_____

_____

_____

_____

_____

_____

12. What is Jesus' position in the church (see Ephesians 2:20)?

_____

_____

_____

_____

_____

_____

_____

APPLYING THE MESSAGE

13. What is the biggest challenge you face when it comes to living at peace with others?

_____

_____

_____

_____

_____

_____

14. What are you doing to create more unity and peace in your church?

_____

_____

_____

_____

_____

REFLECTING ON THE MEANING

In this section of the letter of Ephesians, the apostle Paul provides us with a summary of what God intends the church—the unified body of all believers—to represent on this earth. First, *the church should represent a new fellowship*. Paul writes, "Now, therefore, you are no longer strangers and foreigners, but fellow citizens" (2:19). In the past, the Gentiles were considered "outsiders" to God's plan for His people, the Israelites. But in Christ, the Gentiles now enjoy a new citizenship. They are no longer on the outside looking in. All followers of Jesus are part of a new fellowship.

Second, *the church should represent a new family*. Paul states that we are all "fellow citizens with the saints and members of the household of God" (verse 19). This is a wonderful picture of unity. If we have put our faith in Christ, we can walk into a church and instantly become a part of it because we are all a part of God's family. No matter where we are, we are never far away from family because the family of God is everywhere.

Third, *the church should represent a new foundation*. Paul describes the church as "having been built on the foundation of the apostles and prophets, Jesus Christ Himself being the chief cornerstone" (verse 20). As we have seen, the cornerstone was the most important piece of the foundation. It was perfectly square so the rest of the foundation, radiating out from it, would be perfectly aligned as well. Because the apostles and prophets built the church off the perfection of Christ, the cornerstone, the foundation they laid was solid. As part of this structure, believers are being built into a holy temple—and we are all being fitted and built together.

When we come together as God's people, we represent the church of God—and the Bible says that God dwells in His temple. So, we need to be sure that we are operating in a manner that is worthy of His dwelling. We must continually ensure that we are representing the church to the world as a new fellowship, a new family, and a new (and solid) foundation.

JOURNALING YOUR RESPONSE

What are the benefits you have experienced from serving in your church?

THE GREAT MYSTERY

Ephesians 3:1–13

GETTING STARTED

What comes to mind when you consider the *mysteries of God*?

_____

_____

_____

_____

_____

_____

_____

_____

_____

_____

_____

_____

_____

_____

SETTING THE STAGE

The first major split in the church, known as the "Great Schism," occurred in AD 1054. The break represented the culmination of a number of theological differences that had been brewing for years between Christians in the

East and those in the West. The two groups argued over certain practices in the church, such as whether it was acceptable to use unleavened bread in communion. But the main issue was over authority. The groups differed on whether the pope in the West had the power in the church or whether that belonged to patriarchs in the East.

The breakup served as the catalyst for a number of divisions to follow—including the Great Reformation in 1521 when the Protestant and Catholic churches divided. Today, there are thousands of denominations within Christianity, and most of them developed as the result of a split. They were born out of anger, hostility, and withdrawal between people who claim to follow the teachings of Jesus Christ. This is the same Jesus who prayed that His followers might be brought to complete unity so that the world would know that God had sent Him!

In this next section, Paul expands on his theme of believers living at peace with one another by letting his readers into a "mystery" that God has revealed to him. This mystery is none other than the fact "that the Gentiles should be fellow heirs, of the same body, and partakers of His promise in Christ through the gospel" (3:6). For Paul, ministering to the Gentiles was the focus of his life—a mission that God had called him to fulfill.

After years of serving Christ, the apostle was still amazed that God had extended to him—"the least of all the saints" (verse 8)—the gift of His salvation. This "mystery" of God's grace had been revealed to him, and now he was compelled to share that message to the world. For all have been admitted into God's family . . . both Jews and Gentiles alike.

EXPLORING THE TEXT

The Mystery Revealed (Ephesians 3:1–7)

¹ For this reason I, Paul, the prisoner of Christ Jesus for you Gentiles—
² if indeed you have heard of the dispensation of the grace of God which was given to me for you, ³ how that by revelation He made known to me the mystery (as I have briefly written already, ⁴ by which,

when you read, you may understand my knowledge in the mystery of Christ), ⁵ which in other ages was not made known to the sons of men, as it has now been revealed by the Spirit to His holy apostles and prophets: ⁶ that the Gentiles should be fellow heirs, of the same body, and partakers of His promise in Christ through the gospel, ⁷ of which I became a minister according to the gift of the grace of God given to me by the effective working of His power.

---

1. Paul likely wrote this letter while under house arrest in Rome, but he states that he is a "prisoner of Christ Jesus for you Gentiles" (verse 1). Why do you think Paul would identify himself in this way? What had his ministry to the Gentiles cost him?

_____

_____

_____

_____

_____

_____

2. Paul now launches into a brief digression about the work God called him to perform. What is the "mystery" that God revealed to him (see verses 3–6)? Why does Paul include this digression in light of what he has just said about the need for peace among believers?

_____

_____

_____

_____

_____

Purpose of the Mystery (Ephesians 3:8–13)

⁸ To me, who am less than the least of all the saints, this grace was given, that I should preach among the Gentiles the unsearchable riches of Christ, ⁹ and to make all see what is the fellowship of the mystery, which from the beginning of the ages has been hidden in God who created all things through Jesus Christ; ¹⁰ to the intent that now the manifold wisdom of God might be made known by the church to the principalities and powers in the heavenly places, ¹¹ according to the eternal purpose which He accomplished in Christ Jesus our Lord, ¹² in whom we have boldness and access with confidence through faith in Him. ¹³ Therefore I ask that you do not lose heart at my tribulations for you, which is your glory.

---

3. The Greek term that Paul uses for *least* indicates that he viewed himself as occupying the lowest rung on the ladder of saints. In spite of this, God had given him a crucial mission. What was that task that Paul felt so compelled to fulfill (see verses 8–9)?

_____

_____

_____

_____

_____

_____

_____

_____

_____

4. Paul's implication is that even the enemies of God in the heavenly realms (Satan and his demons) are now on notice that God has accomplished his plan of salvation *for all people* (see verses 10–12). How might this have encouraged the believers to continue sharing the gospel? How would this have compelled them to unity in the body of Christ?

_____

_____

_____

_____

_____

_____

_____

GOING DEEPER

Paul notes the "mystery" God revealed to him about the Gentiles being brought into His family and sharing in His promises for the Jews, a mystery which was not known to previous generations. However, God had dropped hints about this future reality through many of the Old Testament prophets. In the following passage from Isaiah, God points to such a future conversion of the Gentiles.

Egypt, Assyria, and Israel Blessed (Isaiah 19:18–25)

18 In that day five cities in the land of Egypt will speak the language of Canaan and swear by the LORD of hosts; one will be called the City of Destruction.

19 In that day there will be an altar to the LORD in the midst of the land of Egypt, and a pillar to the LORD at its border. 20 And it will be for a sign and for a witness to the LORD of hosts in the land of Egypt; for they will cry to the LORD because of the oppressors, and He will send them a Savior and a Mighty One, and He will deliver them. 21 Then the LORD will be known to Egypt, and the Egyptians will know the LORD in that day, and will make sacrifice and offering; yes, they will make a vow to the LORD and perform it. 22 And the LORD will strike

Egypt, He will strike and heal it; they will return to the LORD, and He will be entreated by them and heal them.

²³ In that day there will be a highway from Egypt to Assyria, and the Assyrian will come into Egypt and the Egyptian into Assyria, and the Egyptians will serve with the Assyrians.

²⁴ In that day Israel will be one of three with Egypt and Assyria—a blessing in the midst of the land, ²⁵ whom the LORD of hosts shall bless, saying, "Blessed is Egypt My people, and Assyria the work of My hands, and Israel My inheritance."

---

5. It is difficult to imagine a more surprising image than Egypt and Assyria, the continual oppressors of God's people, seeking and finding the Lord (see verses 18–23). How does this passage connect with Paul's words in Ephesians 3:1–7?

_____

_____

_____

_____

_____

_____

6. Isaiah proclaimed the vision that the apostle Paul also declared (see Ephesians 3:6). What was that vision (see Isaiah 19:24–25)?

_____

_____

_____

_____

_____

It had cost Paul a great deal to reveal this "mystery." Had he been content to just preach to the Jews, or if he had been willing to put the Gentiles on a less equal footing in the church, he would likely not be writing this letter from prison. Of course, this was not the first time that Paul had met hostility from the Jews for preaching to the Gentiles. As Luke records, a similar incident occurred when Paul was ministering in Jerusalem.

Arrested in the Temple (Acts 21:26–36)

[26] Then Paul took the men, and the next day, having been purified with them, entered the temple to announce the expiration of the days of purification, at which time an offering should be made for each one of them.

[27] Now when the seven days were almost ended, the Jews from Asia, seeing him in the temple, stirred up the whole crowd and laid hands on him, [28] crying out, "Men of Israel, help! This is the man who teaches all men everywhere against the people, the law, and this place; and furthermore he also brought Greeks into the temple and has defiled this holy place." [29] (For they had previously seen Trophimus the Ephesian with him in the city, whom they supposed that Paul had brought into the temple.)

[30] And all the city was disturbed; and the people ran together, seized Paul, and dragged him out of the temple; and immediately the doors were shut. [31] Now as they were seeking to kill him, news came to the commander of the garrison that all Jerusalem was in an uproar. [32] He immediately took soldiers and centurions, and ran down to them. And when they saw the commander and the soldiers, they stopped beating Paul. [33] Then the commander came near and took him, and commanded him to be bound with two chains; and he asked who he was and what he had done. [34] And some among the multitude cried one thing and some another.

So when he could not ascertain the truth because of the tumult, he commanded him to be taken into the barracks. [35] When he reached the stairs, he had to be carried by the soldiers because of the violence of the mob. ³⁶ For the multitude of the people followed after, crying out, "Away with him!"

---

7. How did the Jews from Asia twist Paul's teaching in order to stir up the crowd? What did they say Paul had done in regard to the "Greeks" (see verses 27–28)?

_____

_____

_____

_____

_____

_____

_____

8. How did God use certain "Gentiles" to save Paul from the mob (see verses 31–33)?

_____

_____

_____

_____

_____

_____

REVIEWING THE STORY

Paul embarks in this section on a short digression about a "mystery" that God has revealed to him—that the Gentiles are now fellow heirs, fellow members, and fellow partakers with the Jews in the promises of God. Paul points out that this mystery was dimly conveyed through the words of the Old Testament prophets—though no one at that time knew exactly what it meant. Paul states this mystery has now been revealed to even the heavenly places, so that all beings recognize that God's plan of salvation is for all human beings. Paul concludes by encouraging the believers to join with him in sharing this message and to never lose heart.

9. How does the apostle Paul describe his God-given mission (see Ephesians 3:1–6)?

_____

_____

_____

_____

_____

_____

_____

_____

10. How does Paul describe the circumstances of his becoming a minister of the gospel (see Ephesians 3:7)?

_____

_____

_____

_____

_____

_____

_____

_____

11. How does Paul view himself as compared to the others in the church (see Ephesians 3:8)?

_____

_____

_____

_____

_____

_____

12. What does Paul say that Jesus will provide to us when it comes to sharing His eternal purposes to the world (see Ephesians 3:11–12)?

_____

_____

_____

_____

_____

_____

APPLYING THE MESSAGE

13. What encourages you to be confident in sharing the message of God's grace to the world?

_____

_____

_____

_____

_____

_____

14. What can you do to strengthen the spirit of unity in your church?

_____

_____

_____

_____

_____

_____

_____

REFLECTING ON THE MEANING

The fact that God has lofty goals for the church and its members should leave us with three questions to consider. First, _do we long for the unity of believers as the Lord does?_ Jesus prayed "[May] they all . . . be one, as You, Father, are in Me, and I in You; that they also may be one in Us, that the world may believe that You sent Me" (John 17:21). Obviously, we have to protect our doctrine and what we believe to be God's truth. But this doesn't change the fact that there is only one family of God and that He longs for that family to be one.

Second _do we love all members of God's family?_ Jesus said, "A new commandment I give to you, that you love one another; as I have loved you, that you also love one another. By this all will know that you are My disciples, if you have love for one another" (John 13:34–35). God makes it clear we are to love everyone, no matter who they are, or what is the color of their skin, or what is their background, or what is their lifestyle or status. We are to love them. The way in which we love them reflects the way we love God.

Third, _are we looking for ways to reach out to those who might not feel included?_ The family of God is all about inclusion. When we see people come to church who seem to be alone, our first instinct should be to reach out to them and make them feel welcome and wanted. After all, they are our brothers and sisters in Christ. They represent our family.

Journaling Your Response

What can you do this week to make someone you know feel more included in your church?

A PRAYER FOR STRENGTH

Ephesians 3:14–21

GETTING STARTED

What is the most intense prayer that you have ever prayed?

_____

_____

_____

_____

_____

_____

_____

_____

_____

_____

_____

_____

SETTING THE STAGE

Paul began this section of his letter to the Ephesians with a prayer—identifying himself as "the prisoner of Christ Jesus for you Gentiles" (3:1). However, the mention of the word *Gentiles* caused Paul to digress and reflect on how God had revealed to him the "mystery" that these Gentiles were now a part of the Lord's own family. Now, with this explanation behind him, Paul again turns to offering a prayer for the believers—asking that they receive strength.

As followers of Christ, we have all faced situations in which we felt like we were being tested to the end of our endurance. It is likely we have also sensed during those trials that there was something within us carrying us along. Looking back, many of us can say, "I've never felt the presence of the Lord like I did during that time." However we describe it, this is the strength that God gives us in our spirit—the strength of our inner person.

Paul makes it clear that our inner strength is necessary because our outer strength is fragile. The older we get, the more acutely obvious this truth becomes. Yet, as Paul writes in 2 Corinthians 4:16, "We do not lose heart. [For] even though our outward man is perishing, yet the inward man is being renewed day by day." It is the inward person—our soul and spirit—that provides the spiritual strength we need to survive.

If we build our hope on the strength of the outward person, we are ultimately going to lose the war. No matter how fit we may be physically, or how much strength we build to endure, the outward person will always perish in the end. However, if we seek to strengthen the inward person, we can be assured of results that will last. When we seek to build up the inward person through faith in Christ, we are building for eternity.

EXPLORING THE TEXT

Power Through Christ (Ephesians 3:14–19)

14 For this reason I bow my knees to the Father of our Lord Jesus Christ, 15 from whom the whole family in heaven and earth is named, 16 that He would grant you, according to the riches of His glory, to be strengthened with might through His Spirit in the inner man, 17 that Christ may dwell in your hearts through faith; that you, being rooted and grounded in love, 18 may be able to comprehend with all

the saints what is the width and length and depth and height—[19] to know the love of Christ which passes knowledge; that you may be filled with all the fullness of God.

1. Paul states that he bows his knees to the one "from whom the whole family in heaven and earth is named" (verse 15). What do these words convey about the attitude that Paul wants his readers to take when they likewise approach God in prayer?

_____

_____

_____

_____

2. As believers submit to Jesus' presence and authority in their lives, His values and characteristics become more evident in the way they live and work with others. What does Paul ask the Father to grant the community of believers in this passage? How is true comprehension of Christ's love carried out in community (see verses 16–19)?

_____

_____

_____

_____

All Glory to God (Ephesians 3:20–21)

[20] Now to Him who is able to do exceedingly abundantly above all that we ask or think, according to the power that works in us, [21] to Him be glory in the church by Christ Jesus to all generations, forever and ever. Amen.

3. Paul has just finished asking God to grant the believers a deep understanding of the love of Christ. How does he reassure them that God can grant this request (see verse 20)?

_____

_____

_____

_____

4. Paul ends his prayer by stating that God's glory will endure "to all generations, forever and ever" (see verse 21). What is he reminding his readers here about God's sovereignty? What is he stating about God's plans and purposes on earth?

_____

_____

_____

_____

Going Deeper

Like Paul, Jesus made it clear during His ministry on earth that our inner strength comes from Him. As He prepared His disciples for His crucifixion, He assured them that those who love Him and keep His commandments will not only experience His love but also His indwelling presence. The Holy Spirit will reside in such a person—providing wisdom, strength, endurance, and courage.

Indwelling of the Father and the Son (John 14:19–24)

 ¹⁹ "A little while longer and the world will see Me no more, but you will see Me. Because I live, you will live also. ²⁰ At that day you will

know that I am in My Father, and you in Me, and I in you. [21] He who has My commandments and keeps them, it is he who loves Me. And he who loves Me will be loved by My Father, and I will love him and manifest Myself to him."

[22] Judas (not Iscariot) said to Him, "Lord, how is it that You will manifest Yourself to us, and not to the world?"

[23] Jesus answered and said to him, "If anyone loves Me, he will keep My word; and My Father will love him, and We will come to him and make Our home with him. [24] He who does not love Me does not keep My words; and the word which you hear is not Mine but the Father's who sent Me."

---

5. What promise does Jesus make to those who love Him—and who demonstrate that love by obeying His commands (see verse 21)?

_____

_____

_____

_____

_____

_____

6. What sets apart followers of Jesus from the rest of the world? What encouragement does Jesus offer to those who choose to love Him and keep His word (see verses 23–24)?

_____

_____

_____

_____

_____

_____

Jesus wanted His disciples to understand they had this access to God's power because a time was coming when they would be tested in their faith. He knew there was a cost in being His disciple, and He wanted them to be prepared. As the following passage relates, He also desired for them to remember God's promise of strength when those difficult times arrived.

The Coming Rejection (John 16:1–4)

[1] "These things I have spoken to you, that you should not be made to stumble. [2] They will put you out of the synagogues; yes, the time is coming that whoever kills you will think that he offers God service. [3] And these things they will do to you because they have not known the Father nor Me. [4] But these things I have told you, that when the time comes, you may remember that I told you of them.

"And these things I did not say to you at the beginning, because I was with you."

7. Jesus warns His followers about the hatred and persecution that they will endure because of Him. What is Jesus' intent for this warning (see verse 1)?

_____

_____

_____

_____

_____

_____

_____

_____

_____

_____

8. If Jesus had not forewarned His followers of future persecution, they might have thought God's plan had gone awry when those persecutions did come. So what does Jesus want His followers to remember when faced with such persecution (see verses 2–4)?

_____

_____

_____

_____

_____

REVIEWING THE STORY

Paul offers a prayer for inner strength on behalf of the believers. He assumes a kneeling posture as a declaration of his dependence on God. His first petition is for believers to receive inward *power*: the strength, resilience, and stamina they need to persevere. His second petition is for an inward *presence*: for Christ to dwell in their hearts. His third petition is for an inward *perception*: the ability for them to comprehend the breadth, length, depth, and height of God's love. His fourth petition is for an inward *provision*: an experience of the fullness of God in them.

9. What is Paul's attitude of the heart as he begins this prayer (see Ephesians 3:14)?

_____

_____

_____

_____

_____

10. How does Paul describe the love of Christ (see Ephesians 3:19)?

_____

_____

_____

_____

_____

11. How does Paul refer to the Lord (see Ephesians 3:20)?

_____

_____

_____

_____

_____

12. What does Paul say should be ascribed to God (see Ephesians 3:21)?

_____

_____

_____

_____

APPLYING THE MESSAGE

13. What are some areas in your inner life that need to be strengthened?

_____

_____

_____

_____

_____

14. What are some ways that you can strengthen your inner person?

_____

_____

_____

_____

_____

_____

REFLECTING ON THE MEANING

The first thing we notice about Paul's prayer in this section is his posture. He begins by saying, "For this reason I bow my knees to the Father" (3:14). This may not seem unusual at first glance. However, when Jewish people prayed during this time, they didn't bow their knees. They stood upright, usually with their hands uplifted (see Luke 18:9–14).

But Paul writes, "When I pray this prayer for you, I bow the knee." It's a reminder of the intensity of this prayer. Paul was telling the believers by his posture that this was not an ordinary stand-up prayer. In this, he was placing himself in the company of Christ, who knelt down when He prayed for God to spare Him the suffering He would endure (see Luke 22:41); in the company of Stephen, who knelt down to pray as he faced death (see Acts 7:60); and in the company of Peter, who knelt down to ask God to raise a woman to life (see Acts 9:40).

The takeaway is that when we are serious about prayer, we may not always kneel _physically_ but we had better kneel _inwardly_. When we kneel before someone on earth, we are saying that person is greater than us. When we kneel before God in prayer, it indicates we are subjecting ourselves to His will and submitting to His authority over us.

Prayer is our declaration of dependence. Prayer is saying, "Lord, I'm depending on You." It is saying—with the apostle Paul—"Lord, I'm kneeling before You, and I'm going to bring You some petitions. I'm earnest and sincere about these petitions, and I'm offering up my life before You.

I submit to Your authority—have Your will in these matters." Such a prayer has power, for God promises to answer requests made according in His will (see John 14:13).

JOURNALING YOUR RESPONSE

How do you typically approach God when you come to Him in prayer? How can you pray with a posture of dependence?

WALKING IN UNITY

Ephesians 4:1–16

GETTING STARTED

What are some ways that a church can promote unity among its members?

_____

_____

_____

_____

_____

_____

_____

_____

_____

_____

_____

_____

_____

_____

_____

_____

_____

_____

_____

_____

_____

SETTING THE STAGE

So far, Paul has discussed matters of *theology*—expounding on the riches we have received in Christ, reflecting on the mystery of the Gentiles being admitted into God's family, and offering up prayers for wisdom and strength. Now, Paul will move on to discussing matters of *practice*—revealing how the theology he just discussed should be implemented in our lives. He begins this section with a matter that is close to his heart: *unity* in the body of Christ.

As previously noted, this was a crucial matter in the early church for the simple reason that Gentiles were now accepting Jesus as their Lord and Savior. Previously, the church had been comprised of mainly Jewish converts to Christianity. The new influx of Gentile believers brought new problems with it, for it represented a blending of groups from different backgrounds.

Unity is an issue with which we still struggle in the church today. The problem is so acute that some seminaries are now requiring their students to take courses in conflict resolution. The goal for this training is that when graduates begin serving in churches, they will be able to deal with the issues that come up in their local assemblies.

As God's people, it is critical for us to stay united and maintain peace with one another. Disunity in the church might be understandable if Christianity were merely a personal relationship—if it were just a matter of "Jesus and me"—or if it were nothing more than creeds and confessions. But Christianity is more, for it calls us to be a part of the body of Christ and do His work. It calls us to operate as members of God's own family.

In an orchestra, the conductor will have one of the musicians play a note so the other musicians can tune their instruments to it. By focusing on this note and adjusting their instruments accordingly, all the musicians can be sure they are playing in the same key. In the same way, by focusing our lives on Christ instead of ourselves, we can all be sure that we are playing in concert with one another. When our lives are all tuned to Christ, we can be assured that we will be in tune with one another.

EXPLORING THE TEXT

Walk in Unity (Ephesians 4:1–6)

¹ I, therefore, the prisoner of the Lord, beseech you to walk worthy of the calling with which you were called, ² with all lowliness and gentleness, with longsuffering, bearing with one another in love, ³ endeavoring to keep the unity of the Spirit in the bond of peace. ⁴ There is one body and one Spirit, just as you were called in one hope of your calling; ⁵ one Lord, one faith, one baptism; ⁶ one God and Father of all, who is above all, and through all, and in you all.

1. Paul has designated the believers' standing before Christ in the previous section of his letter. He now reveals how the believers should be living in light of this standing. What characteristics will reveal they are walking worthy of their calling (see verses 1–3)?

2. Paul stresses there is *one* Holy Spirit, *one* body of Christ, and *one* hope to which the believers have been called. Why does he emphasize this point? What is Paul hoping the believers will see as it relates to unity in the church (see verses 4–6)?

_____

_____

_____

_____

_____

_____

Spiritual Gifts (Ephesians 4:7–16)

7 But to each one of us grace was given according to the measure of Christ's gift. 8 Therefore He says:

"When He ascended on high,
He led captivity captive,
And gave gifts to men."

9 (Now this, "He ascended"—what does it mean but that He also first descended into the lower parts of the earth? 10 He who descended is also the One who ascended far above all the heavens, that He might fill all things.)

11 And He Himself gave some to be apostles, some prophets, some evangelists, and some pastors and teachers, 12 for the equipping of the saints for the work of ministry, for the edifying of the body of Christ, 13 till we all come to the unity of the faith and of the knowledge of the Son of God, to a perfect man, to the measure of the stature of the fullness of Christ; 14 that we should no longer be children, tossed to and fro and carried about with every wind of doctrine, by the trickery of men, in the cunning craftiness of deceitful plotting,

¹⁵ but, speaking the truth in love, may grow up in all things into Him who is the head—Christ—¹⁶ from whom the whole body, joined and knit together by what every joint supplies, according to the effective working by which every part does its share, causes growth of the body for the edifying of itself in love.

3. Paul acknowledges that though the body of Christ should be unified and function as one, there is some diversity that exists in the church. What is that diversity? What are some of the different roles and responsibilities that God has assigned in the body (see verses 7–12)?

_____

_____

_____

_____

4. What is the benefit of believers serving in these different capacities (see verses 14–16)?

_____

_____

_____

_____

_____

GOING DEEPER

Paul is striking a balance in this section between calling for unity while also compelling the believers to use their different gifts. It appears that an issue in many churches was the belief that certain gifts were better than others, which had led to some believers being held in higher esteem than others . . . which, in turn, had led to issues of pride. This problem was so prevalent that it compelled Paul to also address it in his letters to believers in Corinth and in Rome.

Unity in Diversity (1 Corinthians 12:1–11)

[1] Now concerning spiritual gifts, brethren, I do not want you to be ignorant: [2] You know that you were Gentiles, carried away to these dumb idols, however you were led. [3] Therefore I make known to you that no one speaking by the Spirit of God calls Jesus accursed, and no one can say that Jesus is Lord except by the Holy Spirit.

[4] There are diversities of gifts, but the same Spirit. [5] There are differences of ministries, but the same Lord. [6] And there are diversities of activities, but it is the same God who works all in all. [7] But the manifestation of the Spirit is given to each one for the profit of all: [8] for to one is given the word of wisdom through the Spirit, to another the word of knowledge through the same Spirit, [9] to another faith by the same Spirit, to another gifts of healings by the same Spirit, [10] to another the working of miracles, to another prophecy, to another discerning of spirits, to another different kinds of tongues, to another the interpretation of tongues. [11] But one and the same Spirit works all these things, distributing to each one individually as He wills.

5. What does Paul say is the source of all the spiritual gifts in the church? Why was it important for him to stress this point (see verses 1–6)?

_____

_____

_____

_____

_____

_____

6. Different gifts are given to different members of Christ's body. What are the different spiritual gifts that Paul lists for the Corinthian believers (see verses 8–10)?

_____

_____

_____

_____

_____

_____

_____

_____

_____

_____

_____

_____

_____

_____

Serve God with Spiritual Gifts (Romans 12:3–8)

³ For I say, through the grace given to me, to everyone who is among you, not to think of himself more highly than he ought to think, but to think soberly, as God has dealt to each one a measure of faith. ⁴ For as we have many members in one body, but all the members do not have the same function, ⁵ so we, being many, are one body in Christ, and individually members of one another. ⁶ Having then gifts differing according to the grace that is given to us, let us use them: if prophecy, let us prophesy in proportion to our faith; ⁷ or ministry, let us use it in our ministering; he who teaches, in teaching ⁸ he who exhorts, in exhortation; he who gives, with liberality; he who leads, with diligence; he who shows mercy, with cheerfulness.

7. What warnings does Paul give regarding pride in the church? How are the believers to consider one another (see verses 3–5)?

_____

_____

_____

_____

_____

_____

8. What are the different spiritual gifts that Paul lists for the Roman believers? In what attitude were the believers to use whatever gift they had been given (see verses 6–8)?

_____

_____

_____

_____

_____

_____

REVIEWING THE STORY

Paul pleads for the believers to live according to the high calling they have received and bear with one another in love. He points out four characteristics necessary for unity in the church: humility, meekness, patience, and forbearance. At the same time, Paul acknowledges there is a diversity of gifts in the church—and the believers are responsible for properly using whatever gifts they have received to serve the body. The gifts that God provides should always be used to edify other believers and create unity, intimacy, maturity, and stability in the church.

9. What does it mean to "walk worthy of the calling" that we received (see Ephesians 4:1–3)?

_____

_____

_____

_____

_____

_____

_____

10. What are the different "ones" that Paul mentions to emphasize the unity of the body of Christ (see Ephesians 4:4–6)?

_____

_____

_____

_____

_____

_____

_____

11. How is grace given to each of us (see Ephesians 4:7)?

_____

_____

_____

_____

_____

_____

_____

12. How does Paul refer to Christ in the structure of the church (see Ephesians 4:15)?

_____

_____

_____

_____

_____

_____

APPLYING THE MESSAGE

13. Why is it important not to hold one spiritual gift higher than another? How can you honor the gifts you see in those around you?

_____

_____

_____

_____

_____

_____

_____

14. How can you put your spiritual gifts to use for the benefit of the body of Christ?

_____

_____

_____

_____

_____

_____

REFLECTING ON THE MEANING

In Ephesians 4:2, Paul calls out four characteristics that are necessary for unity in the church. The first is *humility*. To maintain unity in our churches, we have to be humble. From the pastor to the leaders to the congregation, no one can think they are better or more important than anyone else.

Jesus set the example for us. In Philippians 2, Paul reminds his readers that Jesus came from heaven. Yet even though He was equal with God, He made Himself of no reputation and put Himself in the likeness of human flesh. He humbled Himself, even to the death of the cross.

A second characteristic is *gentleness*, which grows out of a spirit of humility. Most people who are humble are also gentle. They are not *weak* but are able to effectively *control* the power they have been given. The Bible states that Moses was one of the meekest people who ever lived (see Numbers 12:3), but he certainly wasn't weak. Jesus also said he was "gentle and lowly in heart" (Matthew 11:29), but He certainly was not weak. When He was arrested, He said, "Do you think that I cannot now pray to My Father, and He will provide Me with more than twelve legions of angels?" (Matthew 26:53) Jesus kept His power under control.

A third characteristic is *patience*. The Greek word translated as *patience* is *macrothumia*. *Macro* means big, large, or long. *Thumia* means temper. So *macrothumia* is a long temper—the opposite of a short temper. In order to have unity, you have to have humility, which leads to gentleness. Gentleness, in turn, leads to a long temper—a willingness to be patient.

The fourth characteristic is *forbearance* with love. Forbearance means to put up with someone. When we are in the body of Christ, that is what we do. We put up with one another. We forbear, and we do it through love. We do not get bent out of shape because somebody does something that is different from the way we would do it.

The people in our church come from all different backgrounds, but we are all members of the body of Christ. As we embody these four traits—humility, gentleness, patience, and forbearance—we become unified. We gain oneness . . . just as God intends for us.

JOURNALING YOUR RESPONSE

What have you found most helpful in dealing with difficult people?

NEW LIFE IN CHRIST

Ephesians 4:17–32

GETTING STARTED

What is the biggest change you have experienced since accepting Christ?

_____

_____

_____

_____

_____

_____

_____

_____

_____

_____

_____

_____

_____

_____

SETTING THE STAGE

Life in the Roman world during the time of the apostle Paul revolved around pagan worship. The city of Ephesus, for example, was structured around worship practices conducted at the Temple of Diana. The entire system was built on immorality, with more than 1,000 priestesses working in the temple as prostitutes.

Surrounding the temple was a quarter-mile perimeter that was designated as a safe zone for criminals. Anyone who committed a crime would be safe from prosecution if they could get to that zone. So, in Ephesus was a vile temple, surrounded by a quarter-mile perimeter of the most dangerous criminals in the ancient world. Such was life in Ephesus.

Yet in the midst of that wickedness was a group of people who had turned their backs on the illicit worship taking place. This group was not alone, for a similar uprising was taking place throughout the cities of Asia Minor as people came to put their faith in Christ. These believers had formed a church—an island of righteousness in an ocean of wickedness.

Certainly, these believers were feeling the strain. Most were hated and despised by their fellow citizens. They were struggling with how to live a godly life while existing in a very ungodly culture. Paul needed to show them that Christianity was a *revolutionary* way of life that involved taking on a new identity and a new heritage. They were now different from the people they had once been—unique, holy, and righteous before God.

EXPLORING THE TEXT

Let Go of the Past (Ephesians 4:17–24)

17 This I say, therefore, and testify in the Lord, that you should no longer walk as the rest of the Gentiles walk, in the futility of their mind, 18 having their understanding darkened, being alienated from the life of God, because of the ignorance that is in them, because of the blindness of their heart; 19 who, being past feeling, have given themselves over to lewdness, to work all uncleanness with greediness.

20 But you have not so learned Christ, 21 if indeed you have heard Him and have been taught by Him, as the truth is in Jesus: 22 that you put off, concerning your former conduct, the old man which grows corrupt according to the deceitful lusts, 23 and be renewed

in the spirit of your mind, ²⁴ and that you put on the new man which was created according to God, in true righteousness and holiness.

---

1. Paul begins by reminding the believers of how they used to act before they came to Christ. How does he describe the life and mind of the unbeliever (see verses 17–19)?

_____

_____

_____

_____

_____

2. What does Paul say had now changed for them? What are the behaviors, attitudes, and actions of someone who has put on the "new man" (see verses 22–24)?

_____

_____

_____

_____

_____

Embrace the New Life (Ephesians 4:25–32)

---

²⁵ Therefore, putting away lying, "Let each one of you speak truth with his neighbor," for we are members of one another. ²⁶ "Be angry, and do not sin": do not let the sun go down on your wrath, ²⁷ nor give place to the devil. ²⁸ Let him who stole steal no longer, but rather let him labor, working with his hands what is good, that he may have something to give him who has need. ²⁹ Let no corrupt word proceed out of your mouth, but what is good for necessary edification, that it

may impart grace to the hearers. ³⁰ And do not grieve the Holy Spirit of God, by whom you were sealed for the day of redemption. ³¹ Let all bitterness, wrath, anger, clamor, and evil speaking be put away from you, with all malice. ³² And be kind to one another, tenderhearted, forgiving one another, even as God in Christ forgave you.

---

3. Paul uses the word *therefore* in this section to show that a changed identity should naturally lead to changed behaviors. What are the believers to put away (see verses 25–29)?

_____

_____

_____

_____

4. What does it mean to "grieve the Holy Spirit of God" (verse 30)? How are believers to instead treat one another (see verses 31–32)?

_____

_____

_____

_____

GOING DEEPER

Paul wanted his readers to understand the remarkable transformation that had occurred when they accepted Christ. They had received a new inheritance (see 1:11), had moved from death to life (see 2:1), and could now partake in the promises of God (see 3:6). But the believers needed to *live* in light of this new identity and put off their former ways—what Paul calls "the old man" (4:22). In the letter of Hebrews, we find the author making a similar call to his readers.

Run the Race (Hebrews 12:1–2)

[1] Therefore we also, since we are surrounded by so great a cloud of witnesses, let us lay aside every weight, and the sin which so easily ensnares us, and let us run with endurance the race that is set before us, [2] looking unto Jesus, the author and finisher of our faith, who for the joy that was set before Him endured the cross, despising the shame, and has sat down at the right hand of the throne of God.

5. How does the author of Hebrews use the analogy of a runner to describe the way we should live out our faith? What characteristics are required to accomplish this (see verse 1)?

_____

_____

_____

_____

6. What should be our focus as we strive to live a godly life (see verse 2)?

_____

_____

_____

_____

Follow the Straight Path (Hebrews 12:12–17)

[12] Therefore strengthen the hands which hang down, and the feeble knees, [13] and make straight paths for your feet, so that what is lame may not be dislocated, but rather be healed.

¹⁴ Pursue peace with all people, and holiness, without which no one will see the Lord: ¹⁵ looking carefully lest anyone fall short of the grace of God; lest any root of bitterness springing up cause trouble, and by this many become defiled; ¹⁶ lest there be any fornicator or profane person like Esau, who for one morsel of food sold his birthright. ¹⁷ For you know that afterward, when he wanted to inherit the blessing, he was rejected, for he found no place for repentance, though he sought it diligently with tears.

---

7. The author of Hebrews—like the apostle Paul—calls for believers to "make straight paths" and live according to the high calling they received. What are some of the traits that a person who is following God's straight path will possess (see verses 12–15)?

_____

_____

_____

_____

_____

8. The author of Hebrews recalls the story of Jacob and Esau, where Esau commits the folly of selling his inheritance as the firstborn son to Jacob in exchange for food (see Genesis 25:29–34). What point is the author making by recalling this story (see Hebrews 12:16–17)?

_____

_____

_____

_____

_____

REVIEWING THE STORY

Paul uses the analogy of an "old man" and "new man" to help the believers understand the transformation that has taken place in their lives. He instructs them to put off the old man—the way they used to live before finding salvation in Christ—and embrace their new life represented by the new man. As they do this, their minds will be renewed, and they will walk in true righteousness and holiness. Paul closes by emphasizing five areas in which they are to be unique from the world—in their morality (speak truth), their moods (don't be angry), their money (don't steal), their mouths (don't use corrupt speech), and their manners (be kind).

9. According to Paul, how did the rest of the Gentiles—the ones who embraced the Greek and Roman religions—lead their lives (see Ephesians 4:18)?

_____

_____

_____

_____

_____

_____

10. What had these Gentiles given themselves over to pursuing (see Ephesians 4:19)?

_____

_____

_____

_____

_____

_____

_____

11. Why is it important to speak truth with our neighbor (see Ephesians 4:25)?

_____

_____

_____

_____

_____

12. What kind of words should proceed from our mouths (see Ephesians 4:29)?

_____

_____

_____

_____

_____

APPLYING THE MESSAGE

13. What are some traits of the "old man" that you still need to put behind you?

_____

_____

_____

_____

_____

_____

14. How are you seeking to "put on the new man" each and every day?

_____

_____

_____

_____

_____

REFLECTING ON THE MEANING

In this practical teaching from Paul, he highlights three changes that will happen in our lives when we truly put off the "old man" of our former lives and embrace the "new man" in Christ. First, *we will have a new connection to Christ.* The old man was spiritually disconnected and alienated from God. The new man has a relationship with God. The new man knows Christ.

Second, *we will have a new conviction in Christ.* Paul writes, "You have heard [Christ] and have been taught by Him . . . the truth is in Jesus" (4:21). Putting on the new man has to be an experience just as decisive as taking off the old. We have to come to the place where we say, "Lord, You saved me, and I am through with the immorality and sins that were part of my life before I became a Christian. I choose to put on the new man."

Third, *we will be a new creation in Christ.* Paul's point is that there is a vast difference between the way we used to live and the way we are supposed to live. We need to get both feet over to the new side and stop straddling the line to the old one. We must rid ourselves of the things that are tied to who we were before we became Christians. We are to walk in victory so people will know there is something new and different about us.

The key to putting off the old and putting on the new is to "be renewed in the spirit" of our minds (4:23). We have to be consciously inputting godly principles and righteous truths into our minds. This happens as we study the Word of God—replacing old thoughts with God-given ones. The Word of God can wash our minds and cleanse our hearts.

JOURNALING YOUR RESPONSE

Which spiritual disciplines are you using to expel the old and embrace the new?

WALKING IN LOVE

Ephesians 5:1–14

GETTING STARTED

Whom did you try to imitate when you were young?

_____

_____

_____

_____

_____

_____

_____

_____

_____

_____

_____

SETTING THE STAGE

Benjamin Franklin faced a challenge in Philadelphia. He needed to persuade the people of the city to get serious about lighting the areas outside of their houses. The city was facing a darkness-related crisis, not only in terms of crime (which spiked when the sun went down), but also with public safety. People were stumbling and hurting themselves in the streets.

Even though Franklin organized an impressive campaign to get the citizens of Philadelphia to take responsibility for lighting the areas outside their houses, he was getting nowhere. No one was doing anything. Franklin grew frustrated. Then one day, he got an idea. He attached a kerosene lamp to a pole, raised it in front of his house, and lit the lamp. That night, in the city of Philadelphia, there was one house whose exterior was illuminated. The lamp in Benjamin Franklin's front yard cast a warm glow all around his house.

People who walked past the house reported feeling a sense of well-being and safety—and no one fell. The next night, someone else put a lamp up. The night after that, more people followed. Soon, most people in the city were lighting the exteriors of their houses at night. Benjamin Franklin concluded that what he had tried to do by admonition was impossible, but what he did by example became a powerful persuasion throughout the city.

This idea of setting an example looms large in this next section of Ephesians. As Paul says in the very first verse, "Therefore be imitators of God as dear children."

Exploring the Text

Walk in Love (Ephesians 5:1–7)

¹ Therefore be imitators of God as dear children. ² And walk in love, as Christ also has loved us and given Himself for us, an offering and a sacrifice to God for a sweet-smelling aroma.

³ But fornication and all uncleanness or covetousness, let it not even be named among you, as is fitting for saints; ⁴ neither filthiness, nor foolish talking, nor coarse jesting, which are not fitting, but rather giving of thanks. ⁵ For this you know, that no fornicator, unclean person, nor covetous man, who is an idolater, has any inheritance in the kingdom of Christ and God. ⁶ Let no one deceive you with empty words, for because of these things the wrath of God comes upon the sons of disobedience. ⁷ Therefore do not be partakers with them.

1. The word *therefore* ties Paul's call to imitate God to what came immediately before (see Ephesians 4:32). How are the believers to imitate God? What characteristics are they to adopt now that they are a part of God's own family (see 5:1–2)?

_____

_____

_____

_____

2. The world in which Paul lived is not much different from the world we live in today. What is Paul's warning for those who do not turn their backs on their former ways (see verses 5–7)?

_____

_____

_____

Walk in Light (Ephesians 5:8–14)

8 For you were once darkness, but now you are light in the Lord. Walk as children of light 9 (for the fruit of the Spirit is in all goodness, righteousness, and truth), 10 finding out what is acceptable to the Lord. 11 And have no fellowship with the unfruitful works of darkness, but rather expose them. 12 For it is shameful even to speak of those things which are done by them in secret. 13 But all things that are exposed are made manifest by the light, for whatever makes manifest is light. 14 Therefore He says:

> "Awake, you who sleep,
> Arise from the dead,
> And Christ will give you light."

3. Paul once again stresses the radical transformation that has occurred in the believers' lives now that they are members of God's own family. Where before they walked in darkness, they are now the "light in the Lord." In other words, they have taken on God's own attributes as His family members. How should this affect their actions (see verses 8–11)?

_____

_____

_____

_____

4. Paul notes that believers are to have no association with the unfruitful works of darkness. What are believers instead to do? How is this done (see verses 11–14)?

_____

_____

_____

_____

GOING DEEPER

In this section of Ephesians, the apostle Paul stresses that believers in Christ—as members of God's own family—should naturally take on the characteristics of their heavenly Father. In particular, they should imitate God in the way they *walk in light* and *walk in love*. In the Gospels, we find Jesus offering teachings to His followers on these same two points.

Salt and Light (Matthew 5:13–16)

> [13] "You are the salt of the earth; but if the salt loses its flavor, how shall it be seasoned? It is then good for nothing but to be thrown out and trampled underfoot by men.

¹⁴ "You are the light of the world. A city that is set on a hill cannot be hidden. ¹⁵ Nor do they light a lamp and put it under a basket, but on a lampstand, and it gives light to all who are in the house. ¹⁶ Let your light so shine before men, that they may see your good works and glorify your Father in heaven."

5. Jesus said that His followers should be "the salt of the earth" (verse 13). What point was He making about the way His followers should live and conduct themselves?

6. Jesus also said His followers are "the light of the world" (verse 14). What was He saying about their mission? How does this compare with Paul's teaching on walking in the light in Ephesians 5:8–14?

The Greatest Commandment (Matthew 22:34–40)

³⁴ But when the Pharisees heard that He had silenced the Sadducees, they gathered together. ³⁵ Then one of them, a lawyer, asked Him a question, testing Him, and saying, ³⁶ "Teacher, which is the great commandment in the law?"

³⁷ Jesus said to him, "'You shall love the Lord your God with all your heart, with all your soul, and with all your mind.' ³⁸ This is the

first and great commandment. ³⁹ And the second is like it: 'You shall love your neighbor as yourself.' ⁴⁰ On these two commandments hang all the Law and the Prophets."

---

7. What were the Pharisees attempting to do by asking their question to Jesus? What was their intent?

_____

_____

_____

_____

8. Jesus wanted His followers to imitate Him in the way they loved one another. How would this distinguish them as members of God's family? What importance did Jesus put on this command to love others?

_____

_____

_____

_____

_____

REVIEWING THE STORY

Paul issues a call for his readers to be imitators of God—as His beloved children—in the way they walk in love and light. He states they will be walking in love when they model Christ in the way they forgive one another and refuse to be partakers in the sinful ways of the world. Likewise, they will be walking in light when they model traits such as goodness, righteousness, and truth and refuse to be partakers in the unfruitful works of darkness. Furthermore, as they walk in light, they will be actively exposing the works of darkness to the world. Paul concludes by urging his readers to "wake up" to these truths and model them in their behaviors.

9. According to the apostle Paul, what is not fitting for saints (see Ephesians 5:3–4)?

_____

_____

_____

_____

_____

_____

10. What specific deception does Paul warn the believers about (see Ephesians 5:6)?

_____

_____

_____

_____

_____

_____

11. What does Paul say about the fruit of the Spirit (see Ephesians 5:9)?

_____

_____

_____

_____

_____

_____

_____

12. Rather than having "fellowship with the unfruitful works of darkness," what should believers in Christ do instead (Ephesians 5:11)?

_____

_____

_____

_____

_____

_____

APPLYING THE MESSAGE

13. How can you _walk in love_ this week in the way that you interact with others?

_____

_____

_____

_____

_____

_____

14. How can you _walk in light_ this week in the way that you interact with others?

_____

_____

_____

_____

_____

_____

REFLECTING ON THE MEANING

Paul makes a rather startling statement when he writes that believers in Christ are "light in the Lord" (Ephesians 5:8). Jesus said that He is "the light of the world" (John 8:12), and elsewhere in Scripture we read that "God is light and in Him is no darkness" (1 John 1:5). When people choose to put their faith in Christ, they become members of God's own family and begin to take on His characteristics. They transform from creatures of darkness to beings of light.

As this transformation takes place, it alters our behaviors in three primary ways. First, *we begin to walk in goodness in our relationships with others*. When we accept Jesus as our Savior, we emerge from the darkness of deceitful and destructive relationships and have a new direction in life. We begin to look for ways to pursue goodness for both ourselves and others. We will not achieve perfection in this by any stretch of the imagination, for every one of us is still flawed, even after we come to Christ. But we have the *potential* for goodness in our relationships with others because we have been translated from the darkness to the light.

Second, *we begin to walk in righteousness in our relationship with God*. This has to do with being honest, being open, and doing good works. In 1 Timothy 6:11, Paul wrote, "But you, O man of God, flee these things and pursue righteousness." When we walk as children of light, we are purposeful in pursuing goodness and righteousness. We don't just float along with what is going on in the world. We forge our own path toward godliness in Christ.

Third, *we begin to walk in truth with ourselves*. When we make the decision to pursue what is acceptable to God, we naturally cut ties "with the unfruitful works of darkness" (Ephesians 5:11). We begin to carry ourselves with integrity. We make our word our bond. We love and encourage one another. We make sure that our outward persona reflects our inward person. When this happens, people begin to recognize there is something different about us. They recognize us as God's light-bearers in a dark world—and they are drawn to that light.

JOURNALING YOUR RESPONSE

How can you pursue goodness in your relationships with others this week?

WALKING IN WISDOM

Ephesians 5:15–33

GETTING STARTED

What are some of the wisest choices that you have made in your life?

_____

_____

_____

_____

_____

_____

_____

_____

_____

_____

_____

_____

_____

_____

_____

_____

_____

_____

_____

SETTING THE STAGE

We all have made foolish decisions in our past—some of us in the not too-far-distant past. Few of us like to acknowledge our mistakes, but history shows that wise people embrace their errors and learn from them. Just consider the story of Henry Ford, who founded the very successful Ford Motor Company in 1903 and revolutionized the car industry.

What few people know is that Ford was a part of two previous failed auto companies. The first was the Detroit Automobile Company, which went bankrupt after Ford failed to deliver a working vehicle. The second was the Henry Ford Company, which failed for the same reason. The problem was that Ford was a perfectionist. He would keep tinkering with the cars while the investors grew impatient with waiting. Eventually, they pulled out of his companies.

Henry Ford's first two failures prompted him to bring in a partner who understood the business side of the industry. Ford wisely listened to him, and as a result the company shipped out the Model A car on schedule in 1903. For the next five years, Ford continued to listen to feedback from customers and learn from his mistakes. In 1908, the company released the infamous Model T, which became the most popular car of its time.

Ford's story reveals the incredible value that comes from learning from our mistakes. Wisdom is the great need we have in our lives today. The apostle Paul realized this truth when he wrote his letter to the believers in Ephesus and all of Asia Minor. In this next section, he encourages his readers to imitate God, their heavenly Father, not only by walking in love and walking in light . . . but also by walking in *wisdom*.

EXPLORING THE TEXT

Walk in Wisdom (Ephesians 5:15–21)

---

15 See then that you walk circumspectly, not as fools but as wise,

16 redeeming the time, because the days are evil.

¹⁷ Therefore do not be unwise, but understand what the will of the Lord is. ¹⁸ And do not be drunk with wine, in which is dissipation; but be filled with the Spirit, ¹⁹ speaking to one another in psalms and hymns and spiritual songs, singing and making melody in your heart to the Lord, ²⁰ giving thanks always for all things to God the Father in the name of our Lord Jesus Christ, ²¹ submitting to one another in the fear of God.

---

1. In this passage, Paul addresses the need for Christians to walk in wisdom because they live in a world filled with foolishness and evil. What behaviors does he say Christians should avoid if they want to walk the path of wisdom (see verses 15–18)?

2. When believers allow the Spirit of God to fill them, they are able to engage in Spirit-filled worship with other believers. How does the Holy Spirit work within the dimension of worship to build up a community of believers (see verses 19–21)?

_____

_____

_____

_____

_____

_____

_____

_____

_____

_____

_____

Instructions for Christian Households (Ephesians 5:22–33)

22 Wives, submit to your own husbands, as to the Lord. 23 For the husband is head of the wife, as also Christ is head of the church; and He is the Savior of the body. 24 Therefore, just as the church is subject to Christ, so let the wives be to their own husbands in everything.

25 Husbands, love your wives, just as Christ also loved the church and gave Himself for her, 26 that He might sanctify and cleanse her with the washing of water by the word, 27 that He might present her to Himself a glorious church, not having spot or wrinkle or any such thing, but that she should be holy and without blemish. 28 So husbands ought to love their own wives as their own bodies; he who loves his wife loves himself. 29 For no one ever hated his own flesh, but nourishes and cherishes it, just as the Lord does the church. 30 For we are members of His body, of His flesh and of His bones. 31 "For this reason a man shall leave his father and mother and be joined to his

wife, and the two shall become one flesh." [32] This is a great mystery, but I speak concerning Christ and the church. [33] Nevertheless let each one of you in particular so love his own wife as himself, and let the wife see that she respects her husband.

3. Paul concludes his discussion on walking in love, light, and wisdom with some practical advice on how the believers should apply these teachings to marriage. Paul notes that as Christ and the church are one, so should a husband and wife be one. What conclusion does Paul draw about husbands who love their wives (see verses 28–29)?

_____

_____

_____

_____

_____

_____

4. Christians are the members of Christ's body—a truth that must govern all relationships. What implications does this carry for a Christian marriage (see verses 30–33)?

_____

_____

_____

_____

_____

_____

_____

GOING DEEPER

Paul connects walking in wisdom in this section of his letter with understanding the will of God. This same connection can be found throughout the Old Testament. One of the most prominent examples is found in Psalm 32, where God promises to instruct David on knowing His will.

A Promise of Wisdom (Psalm 32:8–11)

> ⁸ I will instruct you and teach you in the way you should go;
> I will guide you with My eye.
> ⁹ Do not be like the horse or like the mule,
> Which have no understanding,
> Which must be harnessed with bit and bridle,
> Else they will not come near you.
>
> ¹⁰ Many sorrows shall be to the wicked;
> But he who trusts in the LORD, mercy shall surround him.
> ¹¹ Be glad in the LORD and rejoice, you righteous;
> And shout for joy, all you upright in heart!

5. David wrote these verses—spoken by God Himself—at the end of a psalm of thanksgiving. What does God promise to David as it relates to wisdom (see verses 8–9)?

_____

_____

_____

_____

_____

_____

6. David began this psalm with the words, "Blessed is he whose transgression is forgiven, whose sin is covered." In light of those words, what reason do the righteous have for rejoicing (see verses 10–11)?

_____

_____

_____

_____

_____

_____

_____

_____

_____

_____

Paul was not alone in urging believers to walk in wisdom. Other authors of the New Testament picked up on this same theme and urged their readers to seek God's wisdom so they might know His will for their lives. James provided the following guidance on this in his letter.

Profiting from Trials (James 1:2–8)

2 My brethren, count it all joy when you fall into various trials, 3 knowing that the testing of your faith produces patience. 4 But let patience have its perfect work, that you may be perfect and complete, lacking nothing. 5 If any of you lacks wisdom, let him ask of God, who gives to all liberally and without reproach, and it will be given to him. 6 But let him ask in faith, with no doubting, for he who doubts is like a wave of the sea driven and tossed by the wind. 7 For let not that man suppose that he will receive anything from the Lord; 8 he is a double-minded man, unstable in all his ways.

7. James was writing to a group of believers who were being persecuted for their faith and likely confused as to why this was happening to them. What wisdom does James provide to them? What does he urge them to consider about their trials (see verses 2–3)?

_____

_____

_____

_____

_____

_____

_____

_____

_____

8. What does James state that God will do for those who seek wisdom? What are the requirements on the part of the believer for receiving this promise (see verses 5–7)?

_____

_____

_____

_____

_____

_____

_____

_____

REVIEWING THE STORY

Paul urges the believers to *walk in wisdom*, seek to understand God's will for their lives, and be filled with the presence and power of the Holy Spirit. He encourages them to worship the Lord together with psalms and hymns and to give thanks to God for His many blessings. Paul concludes by providing some practical instructions for Christian households. He urges wives to submit to their husbands in the same way as they submit to the Lord and commands husbands to love their wives just as Jesus loved the church and sacrificially gave His life for it. He reminds the believers they are all members of Christ's body—the church.

9. What does it mean to "walk circumspectly" (Ephesians 5:15)?

_____

_____

_____

_____

_____

_____

_____

_____

_____

_____

10. What is the best strategy to avoid being unwise (see Ephesians 5:17)?

_____

_____

_____

_____

_____

_____

_____

_____

_____

_____

_____

11. In what way should wives be subject to their husbands (see Ephesians 5:24)?

_____

_____

_____

_____

_____

_____

12. In what way should husbands love their wives (see Ephesians 5:25)?

_____

_____

_____

_____

_____

_____

APPLYING THE MESSAGE

13. How do you know when you are _not_ walking in wisdom?

_____

_____

_____

_____

_____

_____

14. What are some ways that God has revealed His will for your life?

_____

_____

_____

_____

_____

REFLECTING ON THE MEANING

In this section of Ephesians, the apostle Paul urges his readers to "not be drunk with wine . . . but be filled with the Spirit" (5:18). When people drink alcohol, it gets into their system and begins to control them in a negative way. But when people take in the Spirit of God, He gets into their system and begins to instruct them in ways that lead to positive outcomes.

So, how can we be filled with the Holy Spirit and receive these benefits? First, _we have to desire it_. Many believers are not filled with the Holy Spirit because it has never crossed their minds to ask for such filling. They assume having Him in their hearts is enough. The Holy Spirit, however, wants to be more than a resident. He doesn't want to be just _in_ our lives. He wants to be in control of our lives. He wants to call the shots and tell us what to do and what not to do. He wants to guide us back to the way of wisdom when we go astray.

Second, _we have to denounce sin_. The Holy Spirit is not comfortable abiding in a life that is clouded with sin. For this reason, we must confess our sins to God and receive His forgiveness and cleansing from unrighteousness (see 1 John 1:9). This can be as simple as praying, "Lord God, I want to be filled and controlled by Your Holy Spirit. I want You to reveal any sin that is in my life. I confess it to You. Cleanse me and make me the person You can control."

Third, we must _dedicate our lives to Him_. The filling of the Holy Spirit is not a one-time event but a life-long process. For this reason, we need to seek God each day and ask for Him to fill our lives and guide our steps.

Our daily prayer must be, "Lord, I am Yours . . . totally Yours." As we do this, God gives us wisdom. He reveals things we would have never seen in our own wisdom and teaches us to walk according to His will.

JOURNALING YOUR RESPONSE

What are some ways you have witnessed the Holy Spirit's instruction in your life?

WALKING IN OBEDIENCE

Ephesians 6:1–9

GETTING STARTED

What comes to mind when you hear the word *obedience*?

_____

_____

_____

_____

_____

_____

_____

_____

_____

_____

_____

_____

_____

_____

_____

_____

_____

_____

_____

_____

_____

_____

SETTING THE STAGE

Paul has just concluded his teaching on walking in love, walking in light, and walking in wisdom with a call for the believers to apply these principles in marriage. Wives are to submit to their husbands "as to the Lord" (5:22). Husbands are to love their wives "as Christ also loved the church and gave Himself for her" (5:25). In this next section, Paul will extend this instruction to "walk in obedience" to children, parents, bondservants, and masters.

Paul's instructions to this latter group—bondservants and masters—serves as a form of biblical "employee's manual." The word *bondservant* in this context can also be translated as *slave*. Historians have estimated that at the time Paul wrote these words, there may have been as many as six million slaves in the Roman Empire. The vast majority of these slaves were carrying out the business of Rome. They were the farmers, educators, nannies, shopkeepers, and sanitation workers. They were almost everything in Roman culture.

Paul realized many of these slaves were coming to faith in Jesus. He also realized they were experiencing every kind of treatment at the hands of every sort of master. Some of their masters were cruel and heartless, while others were kind and treated them like family. Some of their masters were fellow Christians, while others were actively hostile to the Christian faith. Paul's instructions apply to all these workforce situations . . . and to ours as well.

EXPLORING THE TEXT

Children and Parents (Ephesians 6:1–4)

[1] Children, obey your parents in the Lord, for this is right. [2] "Honor your father and mother," which is the first commandment with promise: [3] "that it may be well with you and you may live long on the earth."

⁴ And you, fathers, do not provoke your children to wrath, but bring them up in the training and admonition of the Lord.

1. Paul is presumably writing to children who are old enough to understand this teaching yet young enough to be under their parents' training. What reason does Paul offer for children to obey their parents? What are the implications of the promise that honoring parents allows a child to "be well" and "live long on the earth" (verses 1–3)?

_____

_____

_____

_____

2. Paul directed his next instruction to *fathers*, given the patriarchal society in which he lived, but this term can apply to all parents. What is this instruction (see verse 4)?

_____

_____

_____

_____

Bondservants and Masters (Ephesians 6:5–8)

⁵ Bondservants, be obedient to those who are your masters according to the flesh, with fear and trembling, in sincerity of heart, as to Christ; ⁶ not with eyeservice, as men-pleasers, but as bondservants of Christ, doing the will of God from the heart, ⁷ with goodwill doing service, as to the Lord, and not to men, ⁸ knowing that whatever good anyone does, he will receive the same from the Lord, whether he is a slave or free.

3. It would have been as difficult for Paul to imagine a world without bondservants as it would be for us to imagine a world without electricity. Bondservants were essential to the functioning of the society of the day. Today, Paul would perhaps address this teaching to employees and employers. How are employees to conduct themselves (see verses 5–8)?

_____

_____

_____

_____

_____

_____

4. Obedience to Christ is the standard by which we measure our dedication to our work. Why must our work as believers be held to such a high standard (see verse 7)?

_____

_____

_____

_____

_____

_____

GOING DEEPER

In this section of Ephesians, the apostle Paul urges children to obey their parents, "for this is right" (6:1). He then proceeds to quote the Fifth Commandment (from the Ten Commandments), noting that it is "the first commandment with promise" (6:2). A quick glance at the Ten Commandments given in Exodus 20 confirms its uniqueness.

The Ten Commandments (Exodus 20:1–17)

¹ And God spoke all these words, saying:

² "I am the LORD your God, who brought you out of the land of Egypt, out of the house of bondage.

³ "You shall have no other gods before Me.

⁴ "You shall not make for yourself a carved image—any likeness of anything that is in heaven above, or that is in the earth beneath, or that is in the water under the earth; ⁵ you shall not bow down to them nor serve them. For I, the LORD your God, am a jealous God, visiting the iniquity of the fathers upon the children to the third and fourth generations of those who hate Me, ⁶ but showing mercy to thousands, to those who love Me and keep My commandments.

⁷ "You shall not take the name of the LORD your God in vain, for the LORD will not hold him guiltless who takes His name in vain.

⁸ "Remember the Sabbath day, to keep it holy. ⁹ Six days you shall labor and do all your work, ¹⁰ but the seventh day is the Sabbath of the LORD your God. In it you shall do no work: you, nor your son, nor your daughter, nor your male servant, nor your female servant, nor your cattle, nor your stranger who is within your gates. ¹¹ For in six days the LORD made the heavens and the earth, the sea, and all that is in them, and rested the seventh day. Therefore the LORD blessed the Sabbath day and hallowed it.

¹² "Honor your father and your mother, that your days may be long upon the land which the LORD your God is giving you.

¹³ "You shall not murder.

¹⁴ "You shall not commit adultery.

¹⁵ "You shall not steal.

¹⁶ "You shall not bear false witness against your neighbor.

¹⁷ "You shall not covet your neighbor's house; you shall not covet your neighbor's wife, nor his male servant, nor his female servant, nor his ox, nor his donkey, nor anything that is your neighbor's."

5. What does the Fifth Commandment reveal about the importance God places on the system of authority that He established in families (see verse 12)?

_____

_____

_____

_____

_____

6. The commandment to honor one's parents applies not only to young children but also to adult children who are responsible for caring for their aging parents. What significance does this commandment carry in a society where youth is prized and old age is dreaded?

_____

_____

_____

_____

Paul was consistent in teaching that children needed to be obedient to their parents. In 2 Timothy, he describes the evils that will be present in the world just before Jesus returns—and among these evils is disobedience. Paul positions _disobedience_ in his list just after _blasphemers_ and just a little ahead of _traitors_, which indicates just how seriously he took the matter.

Perilous Times and Perilous Men (2 Timothy 3:1–9)

¹ But know this, that in the last days perilous times will come: ² For men will be lovers of themselves, lovers of money, boasters, proud, blasphemers, disobedient to parents, unthankful, unholy, ³ unloving, unforgiving, slanderers, without self-control, brutal, despisers of good, ⁴ traitors, headstrong, haughty, lovers of pleasure rather than lovers of God, ⁵ having a form of godliness but denying its power. And

from such people turn away! [6] For of this sort are those who creep into households and make captives of gullible women loaded down with sins, led away by various lusts, [7] always learning and never able to come to the knowledge of the truth. [8] Now as Jannes and Jambres resisted Moses, so do these also resist the truth: men of corrupt minds, disapproved concerning the faith; [9] but they will progress no further, for their folly will be manifest to all, as theirs also was.

---

7. The early Christians staked their lives on the belief that Jesus' death and resurrection had ushered in a new world—the defeat of evil on Calvary and the final defeat that is yet to come. According to Paul, what behaviors will be prevalent in the last days (see verses 2–5)?

_____

_____

_____

_____

8. What dangers do these individuals pose to Christian households? What does Paul advise believers to do when they encounter such people (see verses 5–7)?

_____

_____

_____

_____

REVIEWING THE STORY

Paul begins this final section of his letter by exhorting children to obey their parents. He emphasizes that obedience to parents is a principle of morality, a precept of Scripture, a protection for children, and a promoter of long life. He follows this teaching with an instruction for parents not to discourage their children but to train them in righteousness. Paul then issues instructions to servants (employees) on how to obey and honor their masters. Paul concludes with instructions to masters (employers) to respect their workers, refrain from abusive treatment toward them, and remember they ultimately are under the authority of God.

9. What is Paul's instruction to all children (see Ephesians 6:1)?

_____

_____

_____

_____

10. What are Paul's instructions to all fathers (see Ephesians 6:4)?

_____

_____

_____

_____

11. What is Paul's first instruction to "bondservants," or workers (Ephesians 6:5)?

_____

_____

_____

_____

12. What will workers receive as they offer service to their employers (see Ephesians 6:8)?

_____

_____

_____

_____

APPLYING THE MESSAGE

13. What are some practical ways to show obedience to those who are in authority over you?

_____

_____

_____

_____

14. What are some practical ways that you can show respect to those who report to you?

_____

_____

_____

_____

REFLECTING ON THE MEANING

One of the principles we need to follow if we hope to have longevity in life is to be obedient to our parents. Let's face it: those who rebel against every fabric of control that God has established have already determined to carve out a difficult path in life. Such a course will not lead to a *good* life, for rebellious ways have a tendency to take their toll on a person.

In contrast, according to the Bible, those who follow God's instructions have a better chance of living a reasonably good life, a long life, and a happy life. So, if we are in rebellion against our parents—regardless of whether we are children or adults—we need to get our act together! The almighty God has said that if we want to have a happy, long, productive, and blessed life, we must obey our parents just as we obey Him.

Of course, this is not to imply that parents are always right. All parents make mistakes. Sometimes they make *big* mistakes—and they will have to answer for their actions. But their imperfection does not exempt us of our responsibility to obey them. Obedience is one of the building blocks of the family—and one of the building blocks of culture.

This is the way God intends it, as Paul makes clear. In a home that is filled with the Spirit of God . . . children will be obedient to their parents.

JOURNALING YOUR RESPONSE

How can you better model obedience in the way you live?

PREPARED FOR BATTLE

Ephesians 6:10–24

GETTING STARTED

How can you tell if you are under spiritual attack from the enemy?

_____

_____

_____

_____

_____

_____

_____

_____

_____

_____

_____

_____

_____

_____

SETTING THE STAGE

The apostle Paul began his letter to the Ephesians by reminding his readers that they had been saved from spiritual darkness and brought into the light of Christ. Throughout his letter, he has continued to point out the fact that two sides exist—the *forces of God* and the *forces of evil* that are present in this world. In this final section, Paul brings this theme to a natural conclusion with some practical advice on how Christians should act given this reality.

The truth is that we *all* are in a spiritual battle. Warfare is taking place all around us. The Bible says that we have an enemy whose sole aim is to hurt and discourage us. As Jesus explained, "The thief does not come except to steal, and to kill, and to destroy" (John 10:10). Satan wants to steal life from us and cause us misery and defeat. He will stop at nothing to disturb our minds, deceive our hearts, defeat our lives, and cause us to doubt our faith.

Satan has been employing this strategy from the beginning. There is a long history in the Bible of Satan interfering with and attempting to destroy the work of God. He tempted Adam and Eve to disobey God. He prompted the people of Israel to rebel against God and worship idols. He convinced Peter to deny Christ, caused Ananias and Sapphira to lie to the Holy Spirit, and continually attacked Paul's work in spreading the gospel. So it is no surprise to read that he will attack us . . . no matter how mature we might be in Christ.

Thankfully, Jesus also said, "I will pray the Father, and He will give you another Helper, that He may abide with you forever—the Spirit of truth, whom the world cannot receive, because it neither sees Him nor knows Him; but you know Him, for He dwells with you and will be in you. I will not leave you orphans; I will come to you" (John 14:16–18). God has not left us defenseless in this battle. And as Paul explains in this final section, He has given us spiritual armor not only to stand our ground but also to fight back against the adversary of our souls.

EXPLORING THE TEXT

The Armor of God (Ephesians 6:10–18)

 ¹⁰ Finally, my brethren, be strong in the Lord and in the power of His might. ¹¹ Put on the whole armor of God, that you may be able

to stand against the wiles of the devil. [12] For we do not wrestle against flesh and blood, but against principalities, against powers, against the rulers of the darkness of this age, against spiritual hosts of wickedness in the heavenly places. [13] Therefore take up the whole armor of God, that you may be able to withstand in the evil day, and having done all, to stand.

[14] Stand therefore, having girded your waist with truth, having put on the breastplate of righteousness, [15] and having shod your feet with the preparation of the gospel of peace; [16] above all, taking the shield of faith with which you will be able to quench all the fiery darts of the wicked one. [17] And take the helmet of salvation, and the sword of the Spirit, which is the word of God; [18] praying always with all prayer and supplication in the Spirit, being watchful to this end with all perseverance and supplication for all the saints . . .

---

1. Paul has been imploring his readers to turn away from the sinful ways of the world and live according to the high calling they have received in Christ. Yet he understands that such a way of life will not come without opposition from the enemy. How does he advise believers to prepare for this struggle? Who does he say is our true enemy (see verses 10–13)?

2. What is the purpose of each piece of spiritual armor? How do prayer and the sword of the Spirit help in fighting our spiritual battles (see verses 14–18)?

_____

_____

_____

_____

_____

_____

_____

_____

_____

_____

Closing Words (Ephesians 6:19–23)

[19] And [pray] for me, that utterance may be given to me, that I may open my mouth boldly to make known the mystery of the gospel, [20] for which I am an ambassador in chains; that in it I may speak boldly, as I ought to speak.

[21] But that you also may know my affairs and how I am doing, Tychicus, a beloved brother and faithful minister in the Lord, will make all things known to you; [22] whom I have sent to you for this very purpose, that you may know our affairs, and that he may comfort your hearts.

[23] Peace to the brethren, and love with faith, from God the Father and the Lord Jesus Christ. [24] Grace be with all those who love our Lord Jesus Christ in sincerity. Amen.

3. Just as Paul opened the letter by praying for his readers, he closes by asking them to pray for him. What is his specific request? Why do you think he again reminds his readers that he is an "ambassador in chains" for the sake of the gospel (see verses 19–20)?

_____

_____

_____

_____

_____

_____

_____

4. It is evident from Paul's endearing description of Tychicus (whom he also names in Colossians 4:7–8) that he trusted and valued this "beloved brother." For what reasons does Paul send Tychicus to the believers (see verses 21–22)?

_____

_____

_____

_____

_____

_____

_____

GOING DEEPER

Paul understood that with the high calling he had received of sharing the gospel came the high probability that he would be besieged by the enemy at every turn. However, as he wrote to the Corinthians, he was "not ignorant of [the enemy's] devices" (2 Corinthians 2:11). The Bible provides many insights into Satan's nature and the tactics that he uses to try to thwart God's plans. One vivid example is found in the opening chapter of the book of Job.

Satan Attacks Job's Character (Job 1:6–12)

⁶ Now there was a day when the sons of God came to present themselves before the LORD, and Satan also came among them. ⁷ And the LORD said to Satan, "From where do you come?"

So Satan answered the LORD and said, "From going to and fro on the earth, and from walking back and forth on it."

⁸ Then the LORD said to Satan, "Have you considered My servant Job, that there is none like him on the earth, a blameless and upright man, one who fears God and shuns evil?"

⁹ So Satan answered the LORD and said, "Does Job fear God for nothing? ¹⁰ Have You not made a hedge around him, around his household, and around all that he has on every side? You have blessed the work of his hands, and his possessions have increased in the land. ¹¹ But now, stretch out Your hand and touch all that he has, and he will surely curse You to Your face!"

¹² And the LORD said to Satan, "Behold, all that he has is in your power; only do not lay a hand on his person."

So Satan went out from the presence of the LORD.

5. Peter writes, "Your adversary the devil walks about like a roaring lion, seeking whom he may devour" (1 Peter 5:8). How does this describe Satan's tactics in this passage?

_____

_____

_____

_____

_____

_____

_____

6. What was Satan's goal in seeking to destroy Job physically? How does he describe the protection God had extended (see verses 9–11)?

_____

_____

_____

_____

In the book of Revelation, the apostle John offers us another a glimpse of Satan. This time, the account is both historical and prophetic. In its historical context, the passage describes what happened when Satan and his angels lost the battle in heaven with Michael and his angels. In its prophetic context, it looks forward to the day when Satan will ultimately be defeated.

Satan Thrown Out of Heaven (Revelation 12:7–12)

7 And war broke out in heaven: Michael and his angels fought with the dragon; and the dragon and his angels fought, 8 but they did not prevail, nor was a place found for them in heaven any longer. 9 So the great dragon was cast out, that serpent of old, called the Devil and Satan, who deceives the whole world; he was cast to the earth, and his angels were cast out with him.

10 Then I heard a loud voice saying in heaven, "Now salvation, and strength, and the kingdom of our God, and the power of His Christ have come, for the accuser of our brethren, who accused them before our God day and night, has been cast down. 11 And they overcame him by the blood of the Lamb and by the word of their testimony, and they did not love their lives to the death. 12 Therefore rejoice, O heavens, and you who dwell in them! Woe to the inhabitants of the earth and the sea! For the devil has come down to you, having great wrath, because he knows that he has a short time."

7. John identifies the dragon as "the Devil and Satan" and "the accuser." What event does this passage describe? What happens to Satan after he and his angels are defeated by Michael and his angels (see verse 9)?

_____

_____

_____

_____

_____

8. Jesus defeated death and sin at the cross . . . and the devil knows it. Yet this defeat has only driven him to more frantically deny the truth of what Jesus Christ has accomplished. Why does the devil have "great wrath" on earth (verse 12)?

_____

_____

_____

_____

_____

REVIEWING THE STORY

Paul concludes his letter with a warning that spiritual warfare is real. The war the believers face is spiritual in nature, so they must be equipped with the spiritual armor of God to defend themselves. Paul urges them to take up the breastplate of righteousness, shoes of the gospel of peace, shield of faith, helmet of salvation, sword of the Spirit, and to cover all with prayer. He then asks the believers to pray for him as he continues to share the gospel in spite of the chains and persecution that he faces. Paul closes the letter by affirming Tychicus, the letter carrier, and asking God to give his readers peace, love, and grace.

9. How does Paul say the believers can stand strong against the devil (see Ephesians 6:10)?

_____

_____

_____

_____

_____

10. What does Paul want the believers to pray for on his behalf (see Ephesians 6:19–20)?

_____

_____

_____

_____

_____

11. What is Tychicus's two-part assignment (see Ephesians 6:22)?

_____

_____

_____

_____

12. What are Paul's closing wishes for the believers (see Ephesians 6:23–24)?

_____

_____

_____

_____

_____

APPLYING THE MESSAGE

13. What is a spiritual battle that you are currently facing?

_____

_____

_____

_____

_____

14. What can you do to "weaponize" your prayer life to fight this battle?

_____

_____

_____

_____

_____

_____

REFLECTING ON THE MEANING

The apostle Paul was familiar with the equipment worn by the Roman soldier. Roman soldiers were a constant presence throughout the empire, and Paul had been imprisoned enough times to get a good look at their gear up close. In this final challenge, he draws on this imagery to show that just as a Roman soldier's equipment helps him to stand against attacks and strike against the enemy, the believers' spiritual armor will help them to stand and repel the attacks of Satan.

Paul lists six key pieces of this armor. The first is the _girdle (or belt) of truth_. The truth is our strength and our weapon. Because Satan uses lies as part of his battle plan, we must put on the belt of truth. We must become familiar with the truth of God in His Word.

Second is the *breastplate of righteousness*. In Christian terms, the breastplate is the righteousness of Christ, which is given to believers at salvation. When Satan attacks with accusations against us, we put on the breastplate of righteousness. This allows us to say, "I may not be all that I should be, but in Jesus Christ, I am the righteousness of God. Satan can accuse me all he wants, but before God, I stand as righteous as His Son."

Third are *the shoes of the gospel of peace*. When we wear the shoes of the gospel of peace, we are ready to stand because we know that we are no longer separated from God. We recognize that Jesus' sacrifice on the cross for our sins has reconciled us to the Father. We can stand in the confidence of His love for us and commitment to us.

Fourth is the *shield of faith*. We face spiritual "fiery darts" from our enemy. He shoots ugly memories from our past and thoughts of maliciousness, lust, lies, and rumors. But with the shield of faith, we can say, "I deflect this in the power of the Lord. I refuse to accept this. This is not who I am. I have a clean heart that was bought at the price of Christ's blood."

Fifth is the *helmet of salvation*. Satan will try to attack our minds by chipping away at our confidence in our salvation. The helmet of salvation will protect us from being corrupted by thoughts that we have to do certain things in order to maintain our salvation. It gives us assurance that we are saved solely because of what God has done through Jesus Christ.

Sixth is the *sword of the Spirit*, which is the Word of God. The Bible is *not* our sword. Rather, the Bible is our *arsenal* where all the swords are kept. In the heat of battle, we can pull out just the right word from God to wield against the enemy in that situation. In the Gospels, we read that when Jesus was tempted in the desert, He quoted different passages of Scripture to combat Satan. When He was finished, Satan left Him. This is how the sword of the Spirit works.

A final piece of our spiritual gear that Paul does not include in his metaphor is *prayer*. Prayer is a key weapon that we also need to know how to wield effectively when struggles come our way. As we learn to use each piece of God's spiritual armor—the belt of truth, breastplate of righteousness, shoes of the gospel of peace, shield of faith, helmet of salvation, sword of the Spirit, and prayer—we will find that we are able to withstand the enemy's attacks.

JOURNALING YOUR RESPONSE

Which piece of the armor of God seems the most valuable to you right now—and why?

_____

_____

_____

_____

_____

_____

_____

_____

_____

_____

_____

_____

_____

_____

_____

_____

_____

_____

_____

_____

_____

_____

_____

_____

_____

_____

LEADER'S GUIDE

Thank you for choosing to lead your group through this study from Dr. David Jeremiah on *The Letter to the Ephesians*. Being a group leader has its own rewards, and it is our prayer that your walk with the Lord will deepen through this experience. During the twelve lessons in this study, you and your group will read selected passages from Ephesians, explore key themes in the letter based on teachings from Dr. Jeremiah, and review questions that will encourage group discussion. There are multiple components in this section that can help you structure your lessons and discussion time, so please be sure to read and consider each one.

BEFORE YOU BEGIN

Before your first meeting, make sure you and your group are well-versed with the content of the lesson. Group members should have their own copy of *The Letter to the Ephesians* study guide prior to the first meeting so they can follow along and record their answers, thoughts, and insights. After the first week, you may wish to assign the study guide lesson as homework prior to the group meeting and then use the meeting time to discuss the content in the lesson.

To ensure everyone has a chance to participate in the discussion, the ideal size for a group is around eight to ten people. If there are more than ten people, break up the bigger group into smaller subgroups. Make sure the members are committed to participating each week, as this will help create stability and help you better prepare the structure of the meeting.

At the beginning of each week's study, start with the opening Getting Started question to introduce the topic you will be discussing. The members should answer briefly, as the goal is just for them to have an idea of the subject in their minds as you go over the lesson. This will allow the members to become engaged and ready to interact with the rest of the group.

After reviewing the lesson, try to initiate a free-flowing discussion. Invite group members to bring questions and insights they may have discovered to the next meeting, especially if they were unsure of the meaning of some parts of the lesson. Be prepared to discuss how biblical truth applies to the world we live in today.

WEEKLY PREPARATION

As the group leader, here are a few things that you can do to prepare for each meeting:

- *Be thoroughly familiar with the material in the lesson*. Make sure that you understand the content of each lesson so you know how to structure the group time and are prepared to lead the group discussion.

- *Decide, ahead of time, which questions you want to discuss*. Depending on how much time you have each week, you may not be able to reflect on every question. Select specific questions that you feel will evoke the best discussion.

- *Take prayer requests*. At the end of your discussion, take prayer requests from your group members and then pray for one another.

STRUCTURING THE DISCUSSION TIME

There are several ways to structure the duration of the study. You can choose to cover each lesson individually, for a total of twelve weeks of group meetings, or you can combine two lessons together per week, for a total of six weeks of group meetings. The following charts illustrate these options:

TWELVE-WEEK FORMAT

Week	Lessons Covered	Reading
1	Secure in Christ	*Ephesians 1:1–14*
2	A Prayer for Empowerment	*Ephesians 1:15–23*
3	Alive in Christ	*Ephesians 2:1–13*
4	A Call for Peace	*Ephesians 2:14–22*
5	The Great Mystery	*Ephesians 3:1–13*
6	A Prayer for Strength	*Ephesians 3:14–21*
7	Walking in Unity	*Ephesians 4:1–16*
8	New Life in Christ	*Ephesians 4:17–32*
9	Walking in Love	*Ephesians 5:1–14*
10	Walking in Wisdom	*Ephesians 5:15–33*
11	Walking in Obedience	*Ephesians 6:1–9*
12	Prepared for Battle	*Ephesians 6:10–24*

SIX-WEEK FORMAT

Week	Lessons Covered	Reading
1	Secure in Christ / A Prayer for Empowerment	*Ephesians 1:1–23*
2	Alive in Christ / A Call for Peace	*Ephesians 2:1–22*
3	The Great Mystery / A Prayer for Strength	*Ephesians 3:1–21*
4	Walking in Unity / New Life in Christ	*Ephesians 4:1–32*
5	Walking in Love / Walking in Wisdom	*Ephesians 5:1–33*
6	Walking in Obedience / Prepared for Battle	*Ephesians 6:1–24*

In regard to organizing your time when planning your group Bible study, the following two schedules, for sixty minutes and ninety minutes, can give you a structure for the lesson:

Section	60 Minutes	90 Minutes
Welcome: Members arrive and get settled	5 minutes	10 minutes
Getting Started Question: Prepares the group for interacting with one another	10 minutes	10 minutes
Message: Review the lesson	15 minutes	25 minutes
Discussion: Discuss questions in the lesson	25 minutes	35 minutes
Review and Prayer: Review the key points of the lesson and have a closing time of prayer	5 minutes	10 minutes

As the group leader, it is up to you to keep track of the time and keep things moving according to your schedule. If your group is having a good discussion, don't feel the need to stop and move on to the next question. Remember, the purpose is to pull together ideas and share unique insights on the lesson. Encourage everyone to participate, but don't be concerned if certain group members are more quiet. They may just be internally reflecting on the questions and need time to process their ideas before they can share them.

GROUP DYNAMICS

Leading a group study can be a rewarding experience for you and your group members—but that doesn't mean there won't be challenges. Certain members may feel uncomfortable discussing topics that they consider very personal and might be afraid of being called on. Some members might have disagreements on specific issues. To help prevent these scenarios, consider the following ground rules:

- If someone has a question that may seem off topic, suggest that it be discussed at another time, or ask the group if they are okay with addressing that topic.

- If someone asks a question you don't know the answer to, confess that you don't know and move on. If you feel comfortable, invite other group members to give their opinions or share their comments based on personal experience.
- If you feel like a couple of people are talking much more than others, direct questions to people who may not have shared yet. You could even ask the more dominating members to help draw out the quiet ones.
- When there is a disagreement, encourage the group members to process the matter in love. Invite members from opposing sides to evaluate their opinions and consider the ideas of the other members. Lead the group through Scripture that addresses the topic, and look for common ground.

When issues arise, encourage your group to think of Scripture: "Love one another" (John 13:34), "If it is possible, as much as it depends on you, live peaceably with all men" (Romans 12:18), and, "Be swift to hear, slow to speak, slow to wrath" (James 1:19).

ABOUT
Dr. David Jeremiah and Turning Point

Dr. David Jeremiah is the founder of Turning Point, a ministry committed to providing Christians with sound Bible teaching relevant to today's changing times through radio and television broadcasts, audio series, books, and live events. Dr. Jeremiah's teaching on topics such as family, prayer, worship, angels, and biblical prophecy forms the foundation of Turning Point.

David and his wife, Donna, reside in El Cajon, California, where he serves as the senior pastor of Shadow Mountain Community Church. David and Donna have four children and twelve grandchildren.

In 1982, Dr. Jeremiah brought the same solid teaching to San Diego television that he shares weekly with his congregation. Shortly thereafter, Turning Point expanded its ministry to radio. Dr. Jeremiah's inspiring messages can now be heard worldwide on radio, television, and the internet.

Because Dr. Jeremiah desires to know his listening audience, he travels nationwide holding ministry rallies and spiritual enrichment conferences that touch the hearts and lives of many people. According to Dr. Jeremiah, "At some point in time, everyone reaches a turning point; and for every person, that moment is unique, an experience to hold onto forever. There's so much changing in today's world that sometimes it's difficult to choose the right path. Turning Point offers people an understanding of God's Word and seeks to make a difference in their lives."

Dr. Jeremiah has authored numerous books, including *Escape the Coming Night* (Revelation), *The Handwriting on the Wall* (Daniel), *Overcoming Loneliness, Prayer—The Great Adventure, God in You* (Holy

Spirit), *When Your World Falls Apart, Slaying the Giants in Your Life, My Heart's Desire, Hope for Today, Captured by Grace, Signs of Life, What in the World Is Going On?, The Coming Economic Armageddon, I Never Thought I'd See the Day!, God Loves You: He Always Has—He Always Will, Agents of the Apocalypse, Agents of Babylon, Revealing the Mysteries of Heaven, People Are Asking . . . Is This the End?, A Life Beyond Amazing, Overcomer, The Book of Signs,* and *Everything You Need.*

STAY CONNECTED
to Dr. David Jeremiah

Take advantage of two great ways to let Dr. David Jeremiah give you spiritual direction every day!

Turning Points Magazine and Devotional

Receive Dr. David Jeremiah's magazine, *Turning Points*, each month and discover:

- Thematic study focus
- 48 pages of life-changing reading
- Relevant articles
- Special features
- Daily devotional readings
- Bible study resource offers
- Live event schedule
- Radio & television information

Request *Turning Points* magazine today!

(800) 947-1993
www.DavidJeremiah.org/Magazine

Daily Turning Point E-Devotional

Start your day off right! Find words of inspiration and spiritual motivation waiting for you on your computer every morning! Receive a daily e-devotion communication from David Jeremiah that will strengthen your walk with God and encourage you to live the authentic Christian life.

Request your free e-devotional today!

(800) 947-1993
www.DavidJeremiah.org/Devo

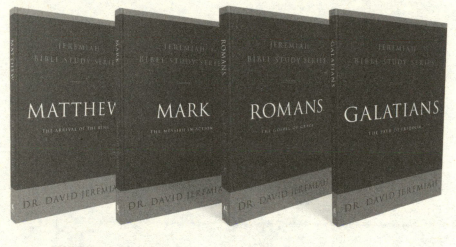

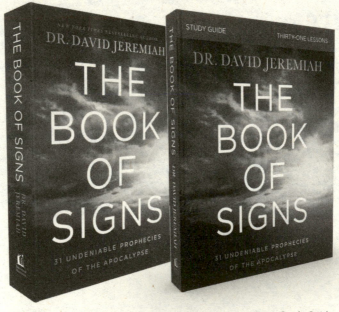

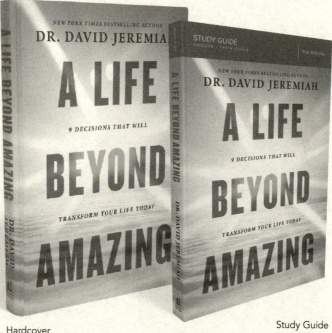